Praise for The Gathering Place

"The Armenian Diaspora has a long history, and even today more Armenians live outside the borders of the Armenian Republic than inside the country. China has also been frequented by Armenian migrants and expatriates throughout recorded history. However, their numbers always remained limited, and the world's most populous country did not become host to a long-established and vibrant Armenian community to attract the attention of historians of Armenian Diasporan communities. *The Gathering Place* promises to rectify that omission. It focuses our attention on a number of colorful Armenian individuals who had escaped in their youth both the Armenian Genocide and the turbulence of the Communist revolution in Russia, found refuge and started a new life in Shanghai, only to endure further hardship during the Japanese invasion, the Second World War and finally the Chinese Civil War."

—Dr. Ara Sanjian, Director, Armenian Research Center, University of Michigan-Dearborn

"A wonderfully vivid and concise history of the triumph and tragedy of the Armenian people through two millennia, combined with the lively and readable narrative of one of its most unique Diasporan communities. *The Gathering Place* is a charming commemoration to both the joy and strength of our culture."

—Kenneth Khachigian

"Armenians will immediately feel 'at home' reading Sergoyan's *The Gathering Place*. Wherever Armenians have migrated, they have rebuilt their ethnic community as soon as they founded a 'club,' which perpetuates their heritage—language, fine arts and literature.

"I was surprised to learn that Armenians migrated East, to Shanghai, for example. Being an Armenian who migrated westward for a new home—as 99% of Armenians did—I had assumed 100% of us went West. This aspect may fascinate other readers, too.

"Sergoyan has recorded the Shanghai Armenians' innumerable contributions; it seems Diaspora Armenians have been valuable everywhere they form communities outside the boundaries of Armenia. Sergoyan is proving the adage, *Once an Armenian, always an Armenian.* Or, wherever an Armenian migrates, he will build a 'club,' where his identity will be born again.

"Shahan Shahnour, a respected Armenian novelist, has said, 'The world will lose nothing if Armenians disappear from the face of the earth. But the world will gain a great deal if Armenians are allowed to survive and make use of their creative powers.' The Armenians of Shanghai have done this."

—Aida Kouyoumjian, author of *Between the Two Rivers: A Story of the Armenian Genocide*

THE GATHERING PLACE

STORIES FROM THE ARMENIAN SOCIAL CLUB IN OLD SHANGHAI

THE GATHERING PLACE

STORIES FROM THE ARMENIAN SOCIAL CLUB IN OLD SHANGHAI

E.G. Sergoyan

coffeetownpress

Seattle, WA

_cp_

coffeetownpress

Published by Coffeetown Press
PO Box 70515
Seattle, WA 98127

For more information go to: www.coffeetownpress.com
sergoyan.coffeetownpress.com

Cover design by Sabrina Sun

The Gathering Place
Stories from the Armenian Social Club in Old Shanghai
Copyright © 2012 by E.G. Sergoyan
Photo of Old Shanghai courtesy of Sherry Mitchell, Old Shanghai Albums

ISBN: 978-1-60381-123-1 (Trade Paper)
ISBN: 978-1-60381-124-8 (eBook)

Library of Congress Control Number: 2012933013

Printed in the United States of America

For Andrenik and Lisa Fay

Table of Contents

Introduction and Acknowledgments   1

Foreword   3

Prologue   5

The Armenian Social Club in Old Shanghai   9

PART I: A JOURNEY ACROSS ASIA – 1912 TO 1937

Chapter 1: The Journey from Baku   21

Chapter 2: The Harbinites   27

Chapter 3: Why Young George Needed to Learn Yiddish 31

Chapter 4: Dairen Quantoon Peninsula   37

Chapter 5: Shanghai Before World War II   43

Chapter 6: War with the Nationalists   49

Chapter 7: "Fey Gee La La"   53

Chapter 8: Shishka and His Gold   57

Chapter 9: The Conte Verde   65

Chapter 10: Adventures with the Clergy   73

Chapter 11: Varak and the Brilliant Spy   81

Chapter 12: The Spy Sorge   85

Chapter 13: Nadia   91

PART II: A FAMILY OF KARS – 1918 TO 1940

Chapter 14: Armenian Origins   97

Chapter 15: In the Time of the Romans   99

Chapter 16: The First Christian State   101

Chapter 17: Armenian Nobility   107

Chapter 18: Haig and Arpenik   109

Chapter 19: Kars, Armenia   115

Chapter 20: The Conscription of Garabed   119

Chapter 21: The Family Leaves Kars (1918)   127

Chapter 22: Aleksander Kolchak   129

Chapter 23: Irkutsk Siberia   131

Chapter 24: The Murders at the Estate (1923)   137

Chapter 25: The Communists in Siberia   141

Chapter 26: The Journey to Manchuria   143

Chapter 27: Manzhouli   149

Chapter 28: The Family Moves to Harbin   153

Chapter 29: Japanese Occupation   157

PART III: THE POST WAR YEARS – 1945 TO 1951

Chapter 30: Working with the American Military   161

Chapter 31: The Chikan Theater   165

Chapter 32: A Long Road to America   169

Chapter 33: Memories of China   173

Chapter 34: The Camp on Tubabao   177

Chapter 35: The Archbishop of Tubabao   179

Chapter 36: The First Run Cinema on Tubabao   181

Chapter 37: Memories of Tubabao   185

Chapter 38: Leaving the Island   189

Chapter 39: Nadia's Vision   193

Chapter 40: Life in the U.S.A.   199

Chapter 41: The Two-Percenters   201

Epilogue   205

Introduction and Acknowledgments

for their contributions.

This book originated as a collection of stories that my parents, relatives and their friends told to their children over the years at holiday tables and gatherings.

Years later, working from a set of audiotapes and notes, I added details and background to give readers a general sense of the era and setting. I recognize that some sections read like travelogues of exotic places while others read like popular history, merely touching on the monumental events that helped shape the modern world. The goal was to spark the interest of future generations who know little about the Old World or the immigrant experience.

I do not pretend to be a scholar of history. I have tried to tell these stories in the voices of the storytellers, in a simple manner that I hope will both educate and entertain. I leave it to others to provide a more scholarly study of the migration of people from Eastern Turkey after the collapse of the Ottoman Empire.

When I contacted friends and family who might corroborate the details and add to the background information, people volunteered more stories. These interviews added even more flavor and new perspectives on the Armenian Diaspora, particularly concerning those who migrated into the Orient.

In writing the book, I benefited from the support of many people. I wish to thank the Ohanjanian family in Canada, the Lukin family in Brazil, the Asryantz family in Russia, the Pashinian family and the Toumanian family in the U.S. for their contributions of pictures and information. I also owe a major debt, which I am happy to acknowledge, to Virginia Meltickian, Edwin

Gerard, Yervand Markarian, and the Western Diocese of Armenian Church for their contributions.

Finally there are three special debts that I wish to acknowledge. First and foremost to my sister, Nina, who plays a part in the stories, helped with the initial drafts, and encouraged the work as it developed; to my publisher, Catherine Treadgold, whose suggestions made the stories more readable and coherent; and as always, to my wife, Lynda, who managed many of the draft details and made it possible for me to concentrate and focus, while suffering my moods and bad manners.

Foreword

The Gathering Place: Stories from the Armenian Social Club in Old Shanghai is many things at once. It is part oral history, part family history, part loving tribute to an intrepid generation that has passed on. It exists somewhere between history and memory. This is not a scholar's archival history, but an account of events as remembered and retold long afterward—a gift of memory from one generation to the next.

The book is based on interviews with Nadine and George, Armenian refugees who made their way to the United States by way of Shanghai during some of the most eventful years of the twentieth century. Nadine and George met and married in Shanghai; in these pages their story is augmented by stories from members of their social circle. Their memories are placed within a rich historical context that illuminates the cosmopolitan nature of life in interwar and wartime Shanghai: Armenian refugees from Turkish oppression encounter Russians fleeing the Bolshevik Revolution and European Jews escaping Nazi persecution. The story of Nadine and George is an extraordinary American story but ultimately it transcends any single place. It helps us see the twentieth century—as much as the twenty-first—as a global century.

—Raymond Jonas, PhD, Professor of History, University of Washington

Prologue

The woman smiled as she looked up from her book and glanced out the window of the observation deck of the third railway car. Visibility outside was zero. The entire terrain outside her train window was what Americans called "a whiteout." Except for an occasional break in the swirling snow, there was nothing to see.

Nadine was smiling at the foul weather because the whole reason for taking the train had been to see the country. She had been raised in Asia and loved the mountains of Siberia, Manchuria and China. As a teenager she would go hiking and rock-climbing regularly with her brother and his friends. She wanted to see the Rocky Mountains of Wyoming and Colorado that she had read about in books and magazines. The writers described the high plains country of America as very *special*, very rugged, unlike anything else in the world. She had only just arrived, yet here she was, in an early winter snowstorm on a stalled train somewhere in Wyoming on her way to Chicago—and there was nothing to see.

She had left San Francisco late afternoon of the previous day to be finally reunited with her family. She was eager to see her children. It had been a year and she feared that her little daughter had already forgotten her. After finally coming to America at the port of San Francisco, she had made arrangements to fly to Chicago overnight and arrive the next day. But her friends had convinced her that the train was far better. "First of all, the train is safer," said her friend Nina. "You can relax, read a book, and watch as the beautiful scenery passes by," she added. "It's really the only way to travel."

Nadine looked out the window again as the train began to speed up and plow through the snowstorm. The only scenery was a few feet past the railway right-of-way. It was hard to believe that the engineer could see anything ahead. But she wasn't particularly concerned. The train she was on was the City of San Francisco—a 'streamliner,' one of the most modern diesel trains of its day. The only disappointment was the severe snowstorm that had hit in the mountains, unusual for early November.

She started to think back on the long journey that had brought her this far. She had been raised in Siberia, educated in Northern China, and had met her husband ten years ago at the Armenian Social Club in Shanghai. She had fond memories of that social club—so many eccentric people, all desperate to escape the war and chaos of Asia. She herself had been separated from her family when they immigrated to America. She had to stay behind in a quarantine ward in a tent camp set up by the United Nations on the Philippine Islands. Only recently had she gotten medical clearance to join her family after a long absence. She would be back with her children soon—just one more day. Hopefully the weather would be better in Chicago.

The observation dome was empty. She rose from her comfortable loungesofa and proceeded to her compartment.

She was in the third car when the trains collided. As the streamliner was derailed, Nadine was propelled across the compartment that was collapsing around her.

In November 1951, here was a blinding snowstorm in the Weber Canyon in the Wasatch Mountains of southwest Wyoming. The conditions were reported to be so bad that the crew of the fourteen-car flyer, City of Los Angeles, another diesel-powered train, had decided to stop in the Weber Canyon. There was traffic ahead and they were unable to see the posted snow-covered safety block signals. Both the streamliner, City of San Francisco and the flyer, City of Los Angeles, were eastbound for Chicago on the same track. They were running approximately thirty minutes apart.

About four miles west of Evanston, Wyoming, the City of San Francisco ripped four car lengths into the City of Los Angeles, first smashing into its observation car and laying it open onto the snow. The other three cars were demolished by the onrushing three-section diesel locomotive. The impact was so severe that it derailed all eleven cars of the City of San Francisco, many of which jackknifed across the right-of-way into a freight train parked on an adjacent siding.

Rescue efforts commenced immediately, considerably hampered by all the snow in the canyon and the freezing temperatures. On the first day, fourteen dead and forty-nine seriously injured passengers and crew were removed from the wreckage. More dead were visible inside the wreckage. It took two full days for rescue workers to cut through the last of the two-train debris with acetylene torches.

Eventually the rescuers came to the conclusion that "there were no more bodies."

The Armenian Social Club in Old Shanghai

There are places in the world that take hold of you and remain with you always. Sometimes these special places can help to shape the way you think and act and react to others because of the people who gathered there. These places can be uncommon and exotic, filled with people out of the ordinary, people tempered by adventure, but sometimes they can seem plain and nondescript until you think back on them years later. Until you remember the extraordinary people you met and the stories they related, you don't even realize they are special.

All through the ages, back to the days of the Greek philosophers, there have been people who have traveled to places that were described to them as special. They traveled to see gargantuan natural wonders or delicate habitats. They traveled to admire man-made palaces, monuments, cathedrals, ruins and museums that serve as a testament to human ingenuity. These many fascinating places become the settings of shared stories. And whether the storytellers are a group of climbers attracted by natural beauty and challenging obstacles or a group of scholars gathered to speculate about the lessons of life, it is the places themselves that become the story and attract our interest.

There are also places and stories that can define an entire era.

One gathering place in an exotic setting inspired tales whose themes were particularly universal. They involved ordinary people engaged in a struggle to survive and prosper during turbulent times. The travelers to this place were motivated by circumstance rather than wanderlust, so the people became the story, and the settings became an afterthought. They were a generation of perpetual travelers, some succeeding in business and prospering in the turbulence of the times, others overcome by the chaos around them.

The Armenian Social Club is remembered as a simple and ordinary building in an extraordinary city—possibly the most exotic city of modern times. The place may no longer exist as some recall it. Whether remembered accurately or romanticized, the club would have been worth the trip just to meet some of the people who were forced to gather there by the events of their time. These people were interesting for many reasons, especially the two-percenters.

A two-percenter is a person who leaves his home, his fortune and sometimes even his country to create a better life during times of trouble. In any village, town or community, only two percent of the people have the courage, the self confidence and the optimism to leave everything behind and build a business in unfamiliar territories. Even in times of war, famine and chaos, the vast majority of any community will stay where they are, and try to survive in familiar surroundings. Not a two-percenter. The two-percenters will continue to move on, even into the most exotic or difficult settings. Filled with optimism and unchecked bravado, they continue their enterprising ways, fully confident in their abilities. The two-percenters in these stories gathered first in Harbin and then in Shanghai. In each city they formed a population of two-percenters.

They were not the first immigrants to these exotic cities, which were originally built up by rail speculators in Harbin and shipping exporters in Shanghai who came to expand their governments' influence in Asia or seek personal fortunes in a region with weak local governments. But the next wave of immigrants that came to Harbin and Shanghai would very quickly constitute the largest and latest to gather there.

This second wave of undocumented refugees gathered in the first half of the twentieth century in Shanghai in the years after World War I (1918) and before the Communist takeover of the Chinese mainland (1949). During these turbulent thirty years, many people were on the move. And Shanghai was unlike anywhere else in the world.

At that time Shanghai was the most open and least regulated metropolis in the world. And for most of those thirty years, it was under foreign occupation. The very word 'Shanghai' had a connotation of criminal or at least unsavory behavior. In one corner of Shanghai—in the International District, sometimes called the Settlements—there was a small club called the Armenian Social Club.

The place was real, of that there is no doubt. With little effort, it can be found in a registry of clubs that existed in Shanghai during this period. It was set up by the Armenian Relief Society in 1910 as a way station for needy Armenian refugees in Shanghai. Originally it served as a relief center in the free port of Shanghai, to help Armenians escaping ethnic murder and war. It was composed of two adjacent houses on 260 and 269 Rue Maresca, which in modern Shanghai is now called Wuyuan Lu.

Many facts about the club are undisputed. For instance, in 1940 the President of the club was Haig Assadourian, who owned the Jai Alai gaming center in Shanghai. The treasurer was his son-in-law, Eduard Hamamdjian, who owned an Egyptian import/export business and was a regular at the club. When an Armenian priest came from Harbin to perform church services in Shanghai—because there was no official Armenian Church—this is the place where he would set up and deliver the services that the relief society provided on Sundays.

The relief society operated on the upper floors, but the first floor of the main building became a social club where people could meet and enjoy each others' company. It had a stage where ethnic plays and musicals were performed, a dance floor for weekend dances, and a café area open twenty-four hours a day with a Chinese staff in attendance. There was a bar, as well as coffee and pastries from a small kitchen. In the back was a huge backyard and garden.

The second house provided limited lodging for arriving refugees. The relief society would even find jobs, clothing and items of need for Armenians on the move. By the end of World War II, Americans of Armenian extraction were warmly greeted by the Armenians in Shanghai, and the soldiers spent most of their time in the club dancing and gambling.

The Armenian Club was not exclusive and not particularly fancy or well-known by the standards of Shanghai in the 1920s and 1930s. It was nothing like the famous clubs established by the British and Americans. It was just a place for like-minded people to gather and swap stories.

Clubs in Shanghai

According to an old guidebook, All about Shanghai, by H.J. Lethbridge, Westerners in the first half of the twentieth century had no trouble finding fancy clubs in Shanghai where they could amuse themselves in their spare time. They would find their way into many clubs and associations built to cater to various nationalities. Even during the Japanese occupation, the clubs were prosperous.

The Shanghai Club—also in the registry of social clubs—was reputed to have the longest bar in the world at that time (thirty-four meters of old unpolished mahogany). Legend had it the bar was so long that if you put your face on it, you could see the curve of the earth. It had a very restricted clientele (positively racist and sexist in its membership policy). On rare occasions, however, non-British nationals could be admitted to membership.

The Shanghai Club, established in 1865, was known to have hosted a lavish reception for U.S. president Ulysses S. Grant in 1879, when he visited Shanghai as a retired citizen. An honor guard of armed Sikhs stood at the front door, and the basement contained barber's shops, a wine cellar and a bowling alley. There were forty bedrooms on the second and third floors of the building.

By the 1930s the Shanghai Club—located at No. 3, The Bund—enjoyed international fame as a British institution in Shanghai.

There were other lavish clubs as well. The Country Club, on Bubbling Well Road, was purely social. This club had an expansive interior with extensive lawns, flower beds and fountains.

The American Club, on Fuzhou Road, was the center of life in Shanghai for visitors and transplants from the United States. Like the Shanghai Club, it occasionally accepted other nationals for membership. At the American club women were not admitted except on one night, the annual "Ladies' Night."

Then there was the Cercle Sportif François, the French Club. Located on Route Cardinal Mercier, this club had the most cosmopolitan membership of any in Shanghai. The number of women members was limited to forty, with many more on the long waiting list. There was a roof garden for dancing in the summer and, inside, a beautiful and spacious ballroom. During the winter, formal Sunday afternoon tea dances were often held in the ballroom.

The Deutscher Garden Klub—the German Garden Club on Avenue Haig—was the athletic and social gathering place for the German community in Shanghai, with visitors enjoying various privileges.

Shanghai at this time was considered by many to be one of five great, exotic cities of the world. In the wealthy parts of the city, movie stars of the day and millionaires partied in fancy hotels and café clubs. They enjoyed fine dining and lived well. In the Shanghai Club the rich and powerful were always positioned three deep, as close to the head of the bar as possible. The taipans (bosses) would assign underlings to stand at the long bar and hold their places while they greeted friends and colleagues. Your place at the bar was an indication of your status in Shanghai society in that era.

Palaces, Restaurants and Dives in Shanghai

Located just down the street from the Shanghai Club was the Hong Kong and Shanghai Bank on the Bund (at No. 12). It opened in 1925 and was mentioned in the Shanghai Guide of that year as the largest bank of the Far East. No expense was spared in its construction because it would serve not only as a central bank but as a symbol of British financial might. In front of

Along the Bund in 1930

the building was a pair of magnificent bronze lions, similar to those standing before the Hong Kong Bank in Hong Kong, itself a British colony in the Orient.

The Park Hotel, popular with the Nazis and many colorful people of the time, was the tallest building in Asia. It was opposite the race track on Bubbling Well Road.

Also located along the Bund was the Cathay Hotel, today the north wing of the Peace Hotel. It was built in 1930 by Victor Sassoon. The office portion of this structure was called the Sassoon House. Among the companies that maintained offices in the hotel were the Chamber of Commerce of the Netherlands and the Banque Belge pour l'Etranger. The remainder of the structure was the Cathay Hotel itself, which boasted a nightclub under a glass roof.

The Sassoon family (reported to be of Iraqi, Jewish and Armenian extraction) made their fortune importing opium from India to China. But when Victor inherited the business in the late 1920s he realized that times were changing and moved his family business from Bombay to Shanghai to invest in real estate and hotels. He built several of the largest buildings in the Orient at that time on speculation. Sassoon, who was a bachelor, lived in the penthouse of the Cathay. When Shanghai became a financial center in Asia, his gamble paid off and he became one of the most important figures in Shanghai until the Communist takeover forced him to leave the city.

On Central Road was the Handy Bar, run by an American, Jimmy James, late of the U.S. 15th Infantry. After being discharged he stayed on in China and opened two restaurants, both of which flourished under the title, Jimmy's Kitchen.

The Kavkas Night Club and Restaurant on Avenue Joffre was owned and run by Mamikon Kardashian, who had established many profitable businesses during his travels in Asia. After several years, the Kavkas had been sufficiently successful to justify a second restaurant, the Renaissance, directly across the street. It was run by Mamikon's son-in-law, Yervand Markarian. Not as fancy as the Kavkas, it catered to a working class clientele. After World War II both restaurants became very popular with the American military. Eventually the son-in-law, Markarian, would bring the Kavkas to America. Resurrected in Hollywood, California, in the 1960s and 1970s, it became a gathering place for movie stars and celebrities of a new generation.

The most notorious attractions in Shanghai were the clubs and restaurants located in what was then called 'Blood Alley.' Blood Alley was actually Rue Chu Pao-san; by the 1930s it had become one of the most infamous streets of all the world's cosmopolitan centers. As famous as the Kasbah in Calcutta or Piccadilly Circus in London or Times Square in New York, it was more notorious and dangerous than any other and not recommended as a tourist attraction. Just a short walk off Avenue Edward Seventh, it was a thoroughfare entirely dedicated to wine, women, song and any manner of debauchery. The only business of Blood Alley was the easy pickings to be had from the drunks, sailors, soldiers and thrill-seeking civilians, who spent time there in the company of the legion of multi-racial women who worked the district.

Located in Blood Alley were the Palais Cabaret, the Frisco, Mumms, the Crystal, George's Bar, Monk's Brass Rail, the New Ritz and half a dozen other clubs.

The Armenian Club, however, served a different purpose than these exotic foreign institutions. Away from the glamour or notoriety of the city center, the Armenian Club was just a non-descript pair of houses on a quiet street away from the action. It was open to anyone and everyone, though most of the regulars were Armenian, Eastern European or Russian. It offered adequate accommodations for those new to the city and in need of a safe haven. New arrivals could rent a room there for a while as they got familiar with the city. In addition to the bar, dance floor and stage, there were billiard tables, places to play chess and backgammon. It had café tables and a small kitchen. Similar to many clubs of the day, it was not at all glamorous by Shanghai standards. It was rarely the site of any trouble—though there was that incident involving a Scotsman.

The Englishman and the Scot

It was clear to everyone that the English fellow who burst into the club that night was lost. He was also obviously inebriated. Witnesses claimed that he kept walking up to the various tables and asking, "Are you a Scot? Are you a Scot? How about you, are you a Scot?" He seemed to think he was in the

British or American part of the International District. Why else would he expect to find a Scot in an Armenian Social Club?. Although it was generally known that the club was not exclusive and anyone could wander in. It was not uncommon to find a variety of people in the café, and it just so happened that a Scot had come to the club on such a night.

The Scotsman was a small, sturdy fellow, drinking at the bar. Rolling his brogue, he said to the nearby Englishman, "Hey you, I'm a Scot. Arrrre you looking for me, Laddie? What is it do you need?"

The Scotsman had been drinking peacefully at the club and had been no trouble to anyone, although no one knew how he had found his way there. The club did have a reputation among the British and Americans as a quiet place to meet a Russian girl. The regulars were certain that the Brits only came to the club because they were convinced that all Russian women were big bosomed and the Brits wanted to verify the rumors. Not that they came very often.

Before he could say another word, the Scotsman suddenly found himself launched through a window into the garden.

No one knows the reason for this assault other than that the Englishman apparently did not like the Scots. And no one made much of a fuss after the Englishman sobered and agreed to pay for the window. This episode and others like it, plus an occasional fist fight over a girl stolen on the dance floor was as much excitement as the club members could recall.

For the most part, the club was not rowdy or troubled by outsiders. It was most often frequented by refugees who knew each other and had traveled a common road to find the International Settlement of Shanghai. The refugees who gathered there considered themselves unique. They weren't necessarily running away from anything; they were there to conduct business in a strange new land. Many of them had intentionally left everything that was familiar to them and had traveled across all of Asia to come to the Armenian Club in Shanghai.

This spirit of adventure was one of the many reasons that the club was one of George's favorite places.

(World Factbook)

Part I

A JOURNEY
ACROSS ASIA
1912 to 1937

Chapter 1

The Journey from Baku

In 1917 George had a long journey ahead of him. Before he reached Shanghai and took up residence at the Armenian Social Club, he would spend his childhood with his family traversing the whole of Eurasia, Siberia, Northern China and Asia's Eastern seacoast.

His journey started in Baku. George was born in Baku, Azerbaijan, in July 1912. At that time Baku was part of Russia and the largest city in the Caucasus region. It had been seized by Russia after several nineteenth-century wars between Tsarist Russia and the declining Ottoman Empire. The Russians and Ottomans had been in a perpetual struggle to control Baku and the oil regions around the Caspian Sea since the early eighteenth century.

In 1723 Peter the Great of Russia seized Baku after a long siege and left two regiments to control the city. In 1795 Baku was the target of a Persian campaign. Then in 1813, by treaty, most of the Caucasus and Baku was ceded to Russia. The first oil well was drilled in 1846 and oil development was started in 1872. The recovery of oil was so successful that by the beginning of the twentieth century, half the oil reserves of the world had been extracted in Baku.

The quarter of a million population of Baku in 1912 was divided into about forty percent Russian, twenty-five percent Armenian, twenty-five percent Azeri's and the rest, Jews and Iranians. Today the majority of the population of Baku is ethic Azerbaijanis and ninety-four percent practice various forms of Islam. The tumultuous transition from a diverse population in an oil rich metropolis on the Caspian Sea to a single ethnic and religious population affected millions of people in the region. To this day, charges of genocide, massacres and wholesale government-sanctioned displacement ignite passion on both sides of the ethnic divide.

For George and his family in those years prior to and during World War I, the situation was not some abstract political struggle but one that was very personal. They were being swept up in the chaos of the times as old world empires crumbled and modern age warfare changed boundaries.

During World War I (1915-1918), the Ottoman Turks successfully occupied the region to control the Baku oil fields and supply oil to the Germans fighting in Europe. Meanwhile the British and the Bolsheviks were maneuvering to take over the region.

George's grandfather decided that the family should all go to China. He was rightfully concerned for his family's safety. Armenians were an ethnic minority and, like so many minorities, were suspected of cooperating with enemies of the Empire. Many Armenians were indeed sympathetic to the Russians and believed that Tsarist Russia would help them to form an autonomous state separate from the Ottomans. After the October Revolution in Russia, Bolsheviks were making similar promises.

George's grandfather thought that the occupation by the Ottomans would last only a short time—that they would be able to return to their homeland after the Russians took over the region. Again, the patriarch told his son Levon to take the family to Northern China and see what business could be set up. The family would wait until the climate changed in Baku and the grandfather wrote for them to return. If business was good, or if things got worse, the other members of the family could immigrate to safety in Northern China as well.

George was only five years old when he left Baku with his family. He had little memory of the homeland, his grandparents and the extended family there. He was destined never to return. And he never again saw the family members he left behind.

From Baku to Irkutsk (1918)

Traveling to China across Russia was like following the path of an old Jules Verne adventure. The family destination in Siberia was the Russian city of Irkutsk. Irkutsk was the largest city in Siberia and the center of a province. From Irkutsk it would be possible to bribe the local authorities to let the family pass into Northern China. That was the plan.

But just to reach Irkutsk—the last major city in Siberia before going to the China border—required a trip of 3,500 miles by train, ferry boat and wagon. The first step was a train ride to Moscow. There were relatively few restrictions in going to Siberia. It was much more difficult to go west to Europe during World War I because all of Europe was a battlefield. In addition to the international war, the Russian Civil War between the Communist Bolsheviks and the Tsarist White Russians was just getting started.

From Moscow you travel by train to Nijini-Norgorod, then by ferry to Kasan on the Volga. From Kasan you go to Perm, also on the Volga. From Perm you go to Yekaterenburg on the river Tobol; then to Ishim and Omsk near the river Irtych. Now you are on the edge of the Siberian frontier where travel becomes more difficult. By wagon you go to Tomsk and on to Achinsk and Krasnoiarsk near the river Yenisei. Finally to Lake Baikal, which is the deepest lake in the world and the origin of the Angara River. Along the Angara River you can travel by ferry to the city of Irkutsk, deep inside northern Siberia. Even after all that, you are still one thousand miles from Northern China.

George's grandfather gave his son Levon (George's father) $30,000 in gold for expenses and to start a business in China. He told his son to go and see what could be done. After he was established in a business, he would send for the rest of the family.

While traveling through Siberia to China, they had to stop for several days in the city of Irkutsk to make arrangements for the last part of the journey. This was in 1917, and Levon went to see the city with some of his friends. During that time he fell into the hands of gamblers and card sharps. And he didn't come home all day and all night. He had believed he was among friends because one of those card sharps was one of his wife's relatives. The relative was married to his wife's sister. To make a long story short, they cleaned him out, and he lost all $30,000 in gold. When he came home the next day he sat down and cried. He said that he had ruined the lives of his children and betrayed his father's trust.

George was the eleventh child in the family. But by that time, 1917, there were only three left. Some of the children died at birth, some because of childhood disease—Typhus was the most common at the time. Several of the children had stayed behind in Baku with relatives and been swept up by the chaos of the time. At this time many people just "disappeared."

George was traveling to China with his father Levon and his mother Ripsime. There was also a brother, Varak (Vladimir), who was seven years older than five-year-old George, the middle child. The last in the party was Varva, his sister, who was ten.

From Irkutsk to Harbin

After losing the money, the family gathered what they could and proceeded to the city of Harbin in Northern China. A year later they received a devastating message. All their family in Baku had been killed or dispersed. Levon's father had been dragged out of his home and killed in the streets by

Levon (George's Father)

the Turks. This news was relayed to them after their arrival in Harbin in 1918-1919. No further information arrived concerning any of the other family members. Many if not all were presumed to have been killed by the Turks.

Levon had been tasked to establish a business in Irkutsk or Harbin for the entire family. After he lost all the money gambling, he endured the unspoken reproach that he had not only failed the family back home, but made it impossible for them to escape. While waiting for word from Northern China, the family in Baku had stayed too long. The Turks and Kurds confiscated everything and killed anyone who resisted. From then on very little was spoken of the family left behind in Armenia, and George grew up with fading memories of relatives he was never to see again.

The Aftermath of World War I

The Turks had been on the losing side of World War I. So, what was left of the Ottoman Empire was being divided by the Allies, mainly Britain and France. The Communist Revolution had erupted in Russia, sweeping away the Tsarist monarchy. In the spring of 1918, the Bolsheviks encouraged civil warfare and mutiny in and around Baku in order to disrupt the oil supplies and take possession of the region. To gain independence from the Ottomans, an Armenian political coalition called the Dashnak Armenian militia decided to align themselves with the Russians. Armenia had not been an independent nation for hundreds of years and Christian Armenians were regarded by the Muslims in the region as an ethnic minority.

During the infamous March Days, using the support of the Dashnak militia and under the pretext of suppressing Tsarist opposition, the Bolsheviks attacked and massacred thousands of Azeris and other Muslims in Baku. The Dashnak Armenians who were hoping to create an independent Armenian state with help from Russia and Britain were getting reports of Turks and Kurds killing or displacing thousands of Armenians in Eastern Turkey. This seemed a continuation of the displacement and annihilation orders issued by the Ottoman government in 1915 that had resulted in so many deaths. The Dashnaks used these reports to justify taking brutal action against the Muslims in Baku. And for a short time, Baku was under Russian and British control.

The Dashnaktsutiun—as the Dashnaks called themselves—did succeed briefly in establishing an independent Armenian republic. From 1917 to 1920, the party was instrumental in the creation of a fledgling republic. It was even recognized by the American President Woodrow Wilson, who wanted Armenia to be an American protectorate. But the American Congress would not sanction the arrangement. Wilson was able to force Turkey to sign the *Treaty of Sevres,* which recognized an independent Armenian state. To this day Armenians celebrate May 28th as their independence day, based on these events. However the independence was short-lived, the terms of the treaty were ignored and most of the republic fell very quickly under Soviet Communist control. The Armenian state eventually became one of the republics of the Soviet Union.

On May 28, 1918, the Azerbaijani faction of the Transcaucasian Sejm proclaimed the independent Azerbaijan Democratic Republic (ADR). Shortly after that, Azerbaijani forces, with support of the Ottoman army of Islam, led by Nuru Pasha, started their advance on Baku, eventually capturing the city from the loose coalition of Bolsheviks, Dashnaks, Mensheviks and British forces. Thousands of Armenians in the city were massacred in revenge for the earlier March Days. Baku became the capital of the ADR. Two years later, the 11th Red Army invaded Baku and reinstalled the Bolshevik authority. Azerbaijan also became a republic of the Soviet Union.

The Turks had been suspicious of the loyalty of the Armenian minority since 1894, when an earlier campaign of extermination was initiated. World War I provided the Turkish authorities an opportunity for the displacement and annihilation of the entire Armenian population under their control, approximately ten percent of Turkey's overall population. After the war, the killings continued until a new government was formed in Turkey and the treaty to create an Armenian Republic was signed.

With the establishment of a Soviet republic in Armenia (western Turkey) and another Soviet republic in Azerbaijan, as well as losses on the battlefield to the British during World War I, the Ottomans had already lost substantial strategic portions of their Empire.

But by the time this new government took control, a reported 1.5 million Armenians were killed, displaced or converted to Islam. Many regard this as the first genocide of the twentieth century. The fledgling Turkish government, wracked by instability, denied any reports of slaughter, confiscation and deportation. They explained the Armenian displacement under their control as a normal consequence of war.

The Soviets took over the oil rich fields around Baku and occupied the region that included Armenia, Azerbaijan and Georgia. This occupation dashed any hopes for independence, and Armenia remained a republic of the Soviet Union for over sixty years.

Meanwhile, George's father Levon realized they would never be returning home and scraped up whatever he could to open a small restaurant in Harbin. That's how the family began to eke out a living in Northern China. Because the Communists took over most of Asia for many years, the family never did get back to their homeland. While George was growing up in Harbin, he noticed that his father suffered from deep depressions. The hardship of their lives in Harbin and his family's grim fate in Baku weighed heavily on his conscience.

The family soon forgot Baku and became Harbinites.

Chapter 2

The Harbinites

The present city of Harbin evolved from a small village in 1898. The village became important when the Chinese Eastern Railway (KVZhD) set up a station in Harbin as an extension of the Trans-Siberian Railway constructed by Russia. This railway reduced the distance to Vladivostok and created a link to the port city of Dalny (Dalian) and the Russian Naval Base at Port Arthur.

Initially the Harbin Russians were mostly the builders and employees of the Chinese Eastern Railway who had moved to Harbin in order to work on the railroad. At the time, Harbin was not an established city. It had been built almost from scratch by the early settlers. Houses were constructed of wood recovered from the local region, while furniture and personal items were brought in from Russia.

The Russian Harbinites were several generations of Russians who lived in the city during this period. A 1913 record shows Harbin had a total of 68,549 people, most of who were of Russian and of Chinese descent. Displaced Russians were by far the largest population of non-Chinese in Harbin.

Following the Russian defeat in the Russo-Japanese War (1904-05), Russia's influence declined in the region, and many Russians left for Siberia. By 1913, Harbin had become an isolated Russian colony for the construction and maintenance work on the China Eastern Railway.

With the next wave of immigrants during the Russian Civil War, the number of different nationalities in Harbin totaled fifty-three. Along with Russian and Chinese, there were forty-five spoken languages used in Harbin at the time. Only eleven percent of all residents had been born in Harbin.

The Armenian community at its height was about 150 families who had moved there from Irkutsk, Siberia and Manzhouli, which was near the Chinese-Soviet border.

Levon, Ripsime and young George at the
restaurant, 1922

Several thousand nationals from thirty-three countries—including the United States, Germany, and France—had moved to Harbin as well. Sixteen countries established consulates and set up several hundred industrial, commercial and banking companies there. The Chinese also established their businesses in brewing, food and the textile industry. Harbin quickly became the center of northeastern China and an international metropolis.

The Civil War Years

In the decade from 1913 to 1923, Russia went through World War I, the Russian Revolution, and the Russian Civil War. In December 1918, during the Civil War, Harbin was flooded with 100,000 Russian White Guards and refugees. These were mostly officers and soldiers involved in the White movement fighting the Bolsheviks, members of the White governments in Siberia and the Russian Far East. They were both the *intelligentsia* of Russia and ordinary people fleeing from the Soviets.

As a result, in the decade of the Civil War, Harbin held the largest Russian population outside of Russia. The Russians even established a private school system and published Russian language newspapers and journals in Harbin.

A separate Jewish community was formed by Russian Jews fleeing anti-Semitic persecution and later included a colony of German Jews who fled Nazi Germany in the 1930s.

In many ways, Harbin preceded Shanghai as a haven for refugees who were moving east from Europe and Russia and quickly became more European in architecture and style than any other Chinese city. Harbin neighborhoods were reminiscent of European Russia, with wide tree-lined boulevards, European style mansions and art décor. Russian stores were located on streets with Russian names like Ulitsa Kitaiskaya (which means "Chinese Street" in Russian). Except for the sight of an occasional Chinese worker or a Mandarin in a rickshaw, people brought to the city unawares might assume they were in a garden city in Russia. Slowly Harbin formed a culture of its own that included fine foods, quality wares imported from east and west and sold in the shops, and an entrepreneurial spirit not found in Soviet Russia.

Most of the residents were comfortable speaking both Russian and Chinese. The schools made English, Russian, Chinese and French mandatory for all students.

The Bolsheviks had neutralized all opposition in Russia, but socialism was for the most part resisted in Harbin. Except for the railway workers, most of the foreign residents were focused on commerce and a work ethic of individualism at odds with the goals of socialism. By the middle of 1918, the Bolsheviks only operated in Northern China with underground cells. The Chinese Army had rounded up all armed Bolsheviks in Harbin and escorted them back to Siberia.

Despite the danger from gangs of Manchurian bandits in the surrounding countryside and the challenges of a long, harsh winter, Harbin served as a haven for all the refugees rich and poor who were struggling to escape the Soviets and establish businesses in an unrestricted market. However, Soviet pressure on the Chinese Republic was building to return the refugees to Russia.

On September 8, 1920, the Chinese Republic announced that it would no longer recognize the Russian consulates in China. Then, on September 23rd, China ceased relations with representatives of Imperial Russia and deprived Russians of extraterritorial rights. Overnight Russians in China found themselves stateless and without documents. Concern over the Red influence that still operated underground led the Chinese government to take control of all foreign-owned institutions in Harbin, including courts, police, prisons, post offices, and some research and educational institutions.

In 1924, an agreement was signed in Beijing regarding the control of the China Eastern Railway (CER). The agreement stated that only Soviet and Chinese citizens could be employed by the CER. This meant the Harbin Russians had to choose not only their nationality, but also their political identity. Some Harbin Russians took Soviet citizenship out of patriotism and continued to work for the CER. Other Harbin Russians remained stateless and eventually were let go from the CER. Gradually, the national and the political identity of the Harbin Russians split into opposing sides.

George and his family grew up in poorer sections of Harbin during these chaotic times. An energetic boy who often wore short pants in the summer months, he helped in the small family restaurant, which specialized in shashlik (a type of spiced meat on a skewer). He enrolled in the American Missionaries' school in Harbin, run by the Methodists; this is where he learned English. He and his family were often referred to as "Harbin Russian" rather than Armenian. Like so many others, they had to Russianize their last name to better fit into the large immigrant community.

His childhood was relatively free of drama until the day he decided to seek his first job.

Chapter 3

Why Young George Needed to Learn Yiddish

When George was fifteen years old he decided to start working after school to help the family. Rather than work in the family restaurant, he wanted a real job. George never forgot his first job, because it required him to learn Yiddish. Yes, Yiddish, the Jewish dialect unique to the German Jews. There was a Jewish population that had immigrated to Harbin after World War I, mostly from Eastern Europe and Russia. But why a Christian Armenian boy needed to learn Yiddish is a tale that was often told at the Armenian Social Club in Shanghai many years later. The tale provided interesting insight into the times and the character of the boy. It was also the boy's first exposure to a prejudice that was a common part of the fabric of life in that era.

George was looking for a part-time job around the poorer sections of the city within walking distance of their home. One day, while walking by a large building, he saw a sign. The building had a cutlery supply warehouse and distribution business with a large barber shop in one corner. In the shop window a sign said, "Help Wanted, part-time work. Only Jewish boys need apply."

This was common in the late '20s, when ethnic ties united people into enclaves. Communities of that era were clannish and restricted, with little or no mixing or diversity. George, of course, was Armenian, not Jewish. But even as a boy he knew about the Jews.

Some people called them names. Many recommended avoiding them. Among the adults in his community, there were bigots who called the Jews 'rats, untrustworthy, unethical and besides they cheated everyone.' He was told to ignore them: 'don't be seen with them or you'll get into trouble.' More than likely, the feelings were mutual. However, some of the more enlightened recognized them from the Bible as "the Chosen people," an ancient sect with honored traditions. At this point in his life all George cared about was getting a job.

Later in his life, he would seek out Jews for business, trade and as friends, all because of this youthful experience.

In fact, George liked them, what little he saw of them. Even when he was young, he never felt slighted by them; he actually thought they were similar to the Armenians: they loved a bargain and relied heavily on tradition. One of the adages of the day was that if you wanted to see some serious bargaining, you should watch a Jew and an Armenian haggle over the price of a pair of shoes.

Physically, both peoples had pronounced features, prominent noses and near-set eyes. Both also had white skins and their share of fair-haired and blue-eyed among them. Both had developed a talent for languages, artistic gifts and a strong work ethic and business instinct. And both peoples typically loved to perform.

At this time, Harbin's small Jewish population consisted mainly of merchants and businessmen from Europe and Russia. These were the first Jewish people George had ever met. He thought, *Well, why not pretend to be Jewish and see if maybe they will give me the job? What have I got to lose?*

The owner of the barber shop was also the owner of the warehouse that supplied cutlery to the city. The owner needed someone to clean up, move inventory and load and unload the delivery wagon. George walked into the barber shop and asked about the job.

One of the barbers looked him over and asked, "Are you Jewish?"

The boy shook his head and answered, "Armenian."

Surprisingly, the barber laughed with the others in the shop and said, "Close enough."

"Now here is what you must do," he said as he lowered his voice and drew the boy closer. "The owner's name is Eli. But you must address him as 'Reb Eli.' Say it over and over each time he questions you. It will show him respect and make you sound Jewish."

"Do you know any Jewish phrases or words?" the barber asked.

George had heard a few words in the school yard and answered, "I know Sholem" (greetings) "and shmuck," (a pejorative relating a male to his organ).

The barber frowned and said, "Don't say 'shmuck'; it is too vulgar. Say 'schlemiel,' if you want to insult someone you know."

The others joined the conversation and also gave advice on how to handle the boss.

"If he accepts you, we will teach you more words and phrases. But first you must convince him."

The barber walked George into the office, where the owner was busy with papers on a desk. The owner looked up as the barber introduced the boy.

"He wants the job in the window," the barber pointed to George.

George introduced himself as George Sergeeff—the Russianized name the family had adopted as they crossed Russia—and told the owner he was interested in part-time work. The owner asked a few questions and George answered each one with "Reb Eli" as the first words out of his mouth.

Quickly he convinced the owner he could do the work as a part-time employee.

Finally there came the dreaded question, "Now you are a good Jewish boy, are you not?" The owner gave him a stern look. George shrugged.

"I'm guessing your family changed their name to sound more Russian and get by, eh? I don't know your family, but you seem like a fine young man, very respectful. Do you go to Temple every week? Do you speak Yiddish?"

The boy nodded tentatively and said, "My mother is very devout."

He immediately regretted the lie. He was sure the owner would test him with a Yiddish question, and that would be that. But, before the owner could speak further, there was some excitement out front. The owner went to see about the interruption. When he returned, he mumbled something about the "schmucks" who worked for him in the warehouse.

"Maybe they are just schlemiel," the boy responded. The owner laughed and was visibly impressed with the boy's extensive knowledge of Yiddish insults. And so, George was sent to the back of the building to meet some of the other workers and get instructions about his new job.

During the following weeks, George actually learned some Yiddish phrases from the workers who thought it was funny that a Russian (George had a Russian sounding name) had pulled a fast one on the boss. George greeted people with 'Sholem aleicem,' addressed his elders as 'reb' (mister), used expressions like 'Gevalt' (exclamation of surprise), 'schlemiel' (klutz or bungler) and 'mazel tov' (good luck) mixed with Russian, which was his first language. It should be noted that by this time, George already knew how to speak Russian, Chinese, Armenian and English.

When anyone spoke to him in Yiddish, the boy would grunt and nod and use the few phrases he had learned to pronounce, pretending that he was just busy or shy. The other workers watched over him and gave him signals on how to respond. They thought the deception was hilarious and encouraged it.

The worst time was when George had to clean the shop where the owner would appear and talk to the customers. Each time they were together in the shop, the boss would call George over to introduce him to friends and acquaintances; he would brag about the fine Jewish boy he had found to help him. Someone would start to speak in Yiddish or tell a story, and George would have to look to other workers or customers in the store for clues as to whether to laugh or frown. Sometimes he would throw in some Yiddish but mostly he would speak in Russian (after all, he was suppose to be a Russian Jew) and then quickly excuse himself before anyone caught on that he didn't understand much of what was being said. They must have all assumed he was just too shy and respectful to address them as equals. Mostly he just avoided everyone, except the several workers who became his teachers and friends.

Things went on like this for a while and the boy was feeling very bad about the whole business. The owner would brag about how George was a good worker and a good Jewish boy. He would tell customers that George went to Temple every week, "even more often than my own son," and that he would grow into a fine, respectful young man.

Everything would have been fine but George was feeling increasingly guilty about lying. He was getting along fine in the part-time job, but he didn't like fooling the owner, who was a good man and very kind to him. The boy decided to tell him the truth.

"The next time he tries to talk to me in Yiddish, I will tell him I am Armenian and not Jewish," the boy told the other workers. The others told him he was being foolish and would certainly lose his job. He promised the others that he would not mention that they had been aware of the deception. But he was resolute.

"Even if it costs me my position in the shop," he decided. "I just don't want to lie to him anymore. He has been good to me. The next time the owner is in a good mood, I will tell him."

But things went on for a while longer. Each time the boy wanted to confess, his courage would fail him. The other workers kept trying to persuade him to be quiet about the whole thing but George was adamant about telling the owner the truth. He just needed the right moment.

Then one day an opportunity presented itself. The owner decided to celebrate his wife's fiftieth birthday at the establishment so everyone could attend. He organized the party in the warehouse for employees, friends and relatives.

On the day of the celebration, the owner began celebrating early by getting a little bit high on the wine. Young George figured this was the best time to tell him the truth; he would confess that he was actually an Armenian. George waited for the right moment and approached the owner, who was smiling and laughing.

The boy respectfully said, "Reb Eli, excuse me but I must tell you something."

The owner smiled and was obviously very unsteady. He laughed at the boy and asked him why he was so serious during the happy celebration. After

Teenager George (front) and friends enjoying a skating rink

George finally told him that he was not Jewish, he was amazed at how quickly the owner sobered up. The owner was shocked and didn't know what to say at first, and George was sure that this was the end of his job.

"What do you mean you are not Jewish?" the owner demanded. "How can you not be Jewish?"

George explained to him that he was an Armenian born in Baku. His family name was Sarkisian and they had changed it to a Russian name during the trip across Asia.

"I don't understand. It's not possible. What do mean you are an Armenian? You can't be an Armenian, a nice Jewish boy like you. It's just not possible," the owner said, shaking his head.

He was obviously upset. He was getting louder and louder, and some of the employees who had been in on the joke listened carefully to the exchange.

George offered to leave immediately if the owner was upset about him being an Armenian.

But the owner was surprised and said to George, "Leave? Why should you leave? Wait, wait, you are a good worker, a fine young man, and I like you. I think God has sent you to teach me that I need to be more tolerant. That's it, isn't it? This is all just a good lesson for me."

The boy was relieved when he realized that he was not going to be fired. But it was obvious that the owner was still upset. Each time he looked at the boy, the owner would shake his head and start muttering how this was all so confusing. Finally the boy got up some more courage, approached him again and asked, "Are you still upset with me, Sir?"

"No, no, everything is fine," the owner said, "it is just a puzzlement to me how you are not Jewish."

"Why is that?" George asked.

"Well," the owner answered, "how can you not be Jewish and yet speak perfect Yiddish?"

George and the owner both glanced at some of the other workers; they all turned away without a word.

The boy worked for that company for several more years until he left Harbin. The lessons of tolerance, honesty and friendship that he had learned at that first job lasted a lifetime. It influenced his choice of friends, business partners and acquaintances.

Chapter 4

Dairen Quantoon Peninsula

In 1933 George was twenty-one years old. He had grown into a slender, pale man, broad shouldered with large, strong hands and a quick, mischievous wit.

That year, George's father Levon died at the age of sixty-seven in Harbin, China. His mother and sister stayed in Harbin, and George moved to Dairen, Quantoon Peninsula, which was under Japanese jurisdiction. Because of his talent for languages, he found a job in Dairen at the RCA Company.

Japan and Russia had long struggled for control of this rich, strategically important region. Japan tried to seize the Liao-tung Peninsula in 1895 but was forestalled by the Triple Intervention. From 1898 to 1904 Russia dominated this region. As part of the Russo-China alliance against Japan, the Russians built Harbin, the naval base at Port Arthur and the commercial center of Dalny. After its victory in the Russo-Japanese war of 1905, Japan took control of Port Arthur. Dalny was renamed Dairen and the Japanese moved into the southern half of Manchuria.

After the Russians lost the war to the Japanese in 1905, some of this territory was transferred under the Potsdam agreement, which for many years left the Japanese militant and anti-American. They considered the treaty forced on them by President Theodore Roosevelt to be unfair, considering their total victory on the peninsula. Feeling that they deserved more territory, they were bitter about Roosevelt's heavy-handed brokering of this treaty.

The Japanese were able to occupy Manchuria in 1931 because Chinese military resistance had been sapped by civil war. This occupation was an unofficial declaration of war on China and marked the beginning of the Japanese intervention. In 1932 Japan annexed Manchuria and renamed it

Manchukuo. They even installed the former emperor of China, Pu Yi, as the ruler of Manchukuo, then put him under the strict control of the Japanese authorities.

As a young man in Dairen, George joined the RCA Victor Company and learned about projectors, amplifiers and electronics. The job was his first association with Americans and allowed him to improve his command of English. He worked there for five years until the Japanese forced the American company out of business.

This was also about the time that George got his nose broken.

The issue of the broken nose has been the subject of discussion and speculation in the family for years. Not just how the incident happened and why it happened but even the time it happened. None of this is clear. George didn't like to talk about it. There are now two tales about the broken nose, and it is impossible to tell which is real. Both are similar yet have significant differences.

First of all, it is important to note that George was not born with the giant nose he had in Shanghai. In later years, his nose preceded him by several seconds when he entered a room. We are talking about a very large nose, huge. His favorite comedians of the thirties and forties were Jimmy Durante and Bob Hope—both known for unusual and distinctive proboscises. He could do an instantly recognizable Jimmy Durante impersonation. When invited to act in stage performances at the Armenian Club in Shanghai, he would always play the villain or the witch with the giant nose. His nose was often the subject of family conversations, and he used it to great effect when scaring children with a snort and a loud sniff as he chased them around the room.

Yet when you look at pictures of the young boy in Harbin, you see a slight youth with fair complexion, brown hair and dark eyes, quite different from his siblings. Sitting beside his mother and father, he clearly resembles his mother's side of the family. Born in Tiflis, Georgia, his mother was small (under five feet tall), and pale, with delicate features.

The young boy's nose is very like his mother's, quite normal. His father and his older brother are larger men with dark complexions and dark features. The brother has an Armenian profile. The father, Levon, who was born in Baku, was tall, bald with a goatee and a heavy brow.

George's father Levon Sarkesian, was born in Baku in 1866. George's mother, Repsimee Malik-Sarkesian, was born in Tiflis, Georgia in 1880. She was sixteen years old when she married Levon by her father's arrangement. In fact, one evening her father told her to put on a nice dress and announced that her fiancé would be coming to dinner that evening. This was the way of marriage in that generation. Her first sight of her future husband was a tall, thirty-year-old man standing in the parlor with flowers in his hands.

Anyway, whenever people asked him about the broken nose, George's version of the story was that he was walking down the street, and two guys jumped out of an alley. One of them had a large stick or club and struck him in the face across the bridge of his nose. He alleged that they called him a "dirty Jew" and ran away.

The problem with this version is the motive. Although there certainly was openly anti-Semitic sentiment in Asia during this period, George did not look particularly Jewish. There was no reason for someone to strike a stranger walking down the street, unless the incident was a random street crime or an act of violence by a couple of punks. George gave very few details as to how and why it had happened.

Years later his wife, Nadia—who had met George in Shanghai at the Armenian Social club—told a different story. She claimed that this second version was told to her by mutual friends and her relatives. Keep in mind that some of Nadia's friends and relatives were not thrilled at the idea that George was courting Nadia. That may have influenced the telling of this tale.

Apparently, George had been drinking and gambling at a casino in Dairen. He regularly found work in the casinos and frequented them often in his youth. One night he was flirting with a young lady in the casino. They were both laughing and having a good time when a friend took George aside and warned him.

"What are you doing?" the friend asked. "Don't you know that woman belongs to a local gangster? You could get seriously hurt. Those two guys over there in the corner are here to protect and watch over her for their boss. If you keep flirting with her, they will come after you."

George looked over at the two thugs and immediately took the threat seriously. He decided to leave the hotel. The two thugs followed him and cornered him in an alley, where they broke his nose with a club.

Nadia's version of what had happened made more sense. Although her friends had told her the story to discourage her from seeing George, it did not work. They married in 1942 and stayed together for nearly fifty years.

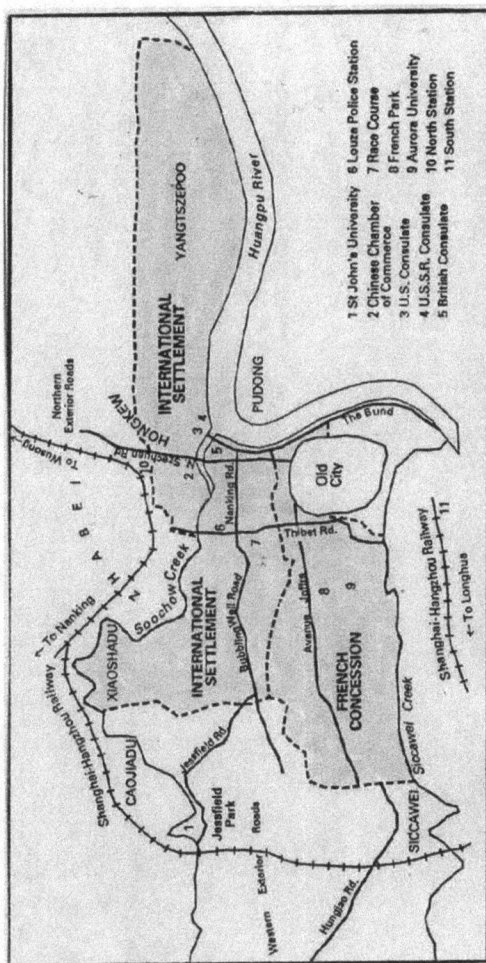

(Tales of Old Shanghai, Maps)

Chapter 5

Shanghai Before World War II

In 1937, when the Japanese forced the RCA Company in Dairen to fold, George moved to Shanghai, where he lived from 1937 until the Communist Chinese Army moved into Shanghai in late 1949. But in 1937, Shanghai was considered the most exciting place in the world.

In the 1930s, this port on the mouth of the Yangtze River boasted some of the most lavishly appointed hotels on earth. The super exclusive Shanghai club was run by the British, who had been in Shanghai longer than any other occupier. Each of the great hotels—the most famous of which were the Palace and the Cathay Hotel—had magnificent architecture and large gambling casinos, and they were *the* destination for movie stars and dignitaries. There were parties at Sassoons, dances at the Cathay, dinners at the Kavkaz, and ballets at the Lyceum Theater. Living in Shanghai, one might not have known that there was a world-wide depression elsewhere throughout the decade.

During the '20s and '30s, Shanghai was a city of exceptional opportunities. Avenue Joffre was the center of the Russian colony in Shanghai and much of the retail trade, restaurants, nightclubs and musical cafes lined the avenue.

The city's location at the mouth of the Yangtze led Shanghai to its development of coastal trade throughout the region. All this became possible because the British insisted on trading silk and tea for opium with the Chinese. When the British won the first Opium War in 1849 and forced opium as a trade commodity on the Chinese, they also insisted on five free ports to handle the trade between Asia and Europe. Gradually the port of Shanghai surpassed the Port of Ningbo and the Port of Guangzhou to become the largest port in China and the largest city in the Far East. Shanghai became the port of call for everyone attracted by elegance and adventure, and the city was transformed into a playground for the rich and famous.

Shanghai may have avoided the world-wide depression because of easy credit. Everything there was based on easy credit. Chinese money was unstable but credit and gold was used with abandon. There were no taxes to speak of and few fees and penalties. China of that period was old world and the old world ran on bribes and connections. Everything was available for a price. Titles, rank, position, business arrangements, licenses and opportunities were negotiable.

The first occupation of China by the Japanese was in 1929, when the Soviets had a confrontation with the Japanese. By 1934, the Japanese began to solidify their occupation of Manchuria. This was, for all intents and purposes, an undeclared war between China and Japan, but the Chinese were in disarray and unprepared to defend themselves. In 1937 the Japanese finally initiated a direct conflict with the Chinese. By this time they had established Manchuria (which they called Manchuko) as a base for further adventures in Asia with the former emperor of China, Henry Pu Yi, as ruler of Manchukuo. And in November 1937 the Japanese occupied Shanghai.

Originally they occupied the Chinese part of Shanghai, called Hongkew. Hongkew was on the other side of the Garden Bridge, which crossed the Whangpoo River. Shanghai was a divided city. Part of the city was made up of an International District or Settlement, and another part was strictly Chinese. The Chinese could come into the International District to work, but afterwards return to their homes across the bridge. For the first half of the twentieth century the District was almost a foreign land inside the city.

The Shanghai International District consisted of various nationalities. There was a Russian section or concession, German concession, American concession, British concession and a French concession. The French concession was considered part of the French empire and separate from the main Settlement. The American and British concessions were combined and run jointly. The area was run by a wholly foreign controlled council called the Shanghai Municipal Council. The council was staffed by representatives of all nationalities from the Settlement. Later a separate Jewish district was created as well, made up of Jewish refugees who emigrated from Northern China or were brought by ocean liners like the Conte Verde, the Conte Rosso and others commissioned to transport Jews from Europe. The Jewish district became known as the Hongkew Ghetto.

The foreigners were the dominant portion of the community and had their own police, who were charged with the order and security of the Settlement. While wealthy Chinese could own property in the District, initially they were not welcome in the Settlement.

Even the parks were closed to the Chinese for many years. Not until 1928 were the Chinese permitted to join the Municipal Council and allowed into the Settlement's public parks. But by 1932 there were an estimated one million Chinese living and working within the International Settlement. At this time the Shanghai population was 2.7 million, making it the sixth largest city in the world.

The downtown area of Shanghai's International Settlement overlooked the western bank of the river. It was known as The Bund (pronounced like 'shunned'), from the Urdu "band," meaning "embankment." The Bund became the Wall Street of Asia, the center of trade and finance. It remains so to this day.

The Bank of Shanghai

Shanghai also had an enormous banking center. By the end of the nineteenth century, it was the world's third most important banking capital after New York and London. It was the financial center of East Asia, with the Bank of Shanghai as its focus. Many wealthy Russians and East Europeans trapped in situations during World War I and the Russian Civil War, who were unable or unwilling to leave their homes, would send their wealth to be stored in the Bank of Shanghai.

One of the bank directors at that time named Wochenkowski told stories of how they would handle these accounts. The bank had a strict policy for all deposit boxes paid in advance and held in secret. The bank directors would hold the accounts open for exactly ten years. At the end of this time, if no claim was made on the account, no heirs with proof of ownership came forward, no contact with the bank about the account was made, then the bank directors would declare the account closed and the contents of the deposit boxes would become the property of the bank.

Imagine the scene in the directors' conference room. All the directors would gather at midnight of the expiration day for a particular account. After the clock ran out at precisely ten years to the minute with no communication from the owners, the directors would declare the contents to belong to the bank, meaning the directors. They would open the box and find treasure and personal wealth that would then be divided among the bank officials and the stockholders.

There were many unclaimed boxes because the circumstances of war often made it impossible for owners to claim their property. Many were killed or imprisoned and the original owners had made no provision for inheritance or care of the accounts. During this chaotic time, the bank directors became incredibly wealthy. This was life in Shanghai during the 1930s.

In Harbin, George's family had tried to establish Chinese citizenship. But late in 1920 the Chinese government declared that it would not recognize their citizenship. Even non-Chinese born in China were considered stateless. And in 1922 the Soviets revoked the Russian citizenship of anyone who had left the country without permission.

Many people, in particular the Russians fleeing the Russian Civil War, moved from Harbin to Shanghai because Shanghai was more stable and had a more robust economy. Also, in the 1930s, more people moved from Manchuria to the coast because of the Japanese occupation, which was becoming brutal.

Most important, Shanghai was a free port. In Shanghai, even though all citizens from Harbin were considered stateless because they didn't belong to any recognized country, Shanghai required no visa, passport or work permit for entry. George had heard all the stories of how much better everything was in Shanghai. So, after his father died, he decided to leave Manchuria and go to Shanghai looking for work.

The First Job in Shanghai

George had many jobs while in Shanghai. When he first arrived, he became an employee in a gambling house. Soon he was trained to work on the tables as a stick man (croupier) or sometimes as a dealer. He mainly worked cards and roulette. Eventually he became a dealer of Baccarat (also called Chemin de Fer). He told tales of watching people winning and losing fortunes at the tables every night. The Chinese loved to gamble. And there were nights when a gambler could amass a huge tower of chips playing cards or roulette and lose it all by the dawn's first light.

There were also times that the big losers would go out into the gardens behind the hotels and commit suicide.

Baccarat was the highest stakes card game of the time, and it was thought to be a game of luck with limited skill required because it was so simple to play. This European game would later become popular around the world as the favorite card game of Ian Fleming's James Bond. You deal Baccarat from a long box called a "shoe," and there were six decks of cards shuffled in the shoe. It was impossible to see the cards or mark them or deal from the bottom. Two cards are dealt to each player with an optional third card. Each deck is shuffled and cut before it is placed in the shoe, and each player is given an opportunity to deal from the shoe. So it is very difficult to gain any advantage.

And yet, every time there was a big winner at the table where George was dealing, the floor manager would tell him to take a break and assign a specialist dealer to the table with the winner. George could never figure out how it was done, but he was sure this dealer was doing something with the "shoe."

By the time the morning sun shone into the casino, the winner had lost all his chips and more. Manipulating roulette was easy and the tricks done to the wheel were common knowledge to employees of the casinos.

The floor manager never told George anything about the Baccarat shoe or the specialist dealer. This was the best kept secret in the gambling houses and he was still new to the business. George didn't stay long enough to discover the secret. For the rest of his life, he did not enjoy card games because of what he saw in the casinos during that fateful first job in Shanghai.

Chapter 6

War with the Nationalists

Fighting between the Chinese and the Japanese began again in 1937 after the Japanese, having occupied Peking, moved toward Tientsin and, in July, occupied that city. New detachments were sent by the Japanese to Shanghai, and an enormous army landed there. It was during this period that the Japanese, without much ceremony, entered the International Settlement with their forces. The invasion was a rare sight; up to now they had left the "Europeans" alone so as not to provoke hostility among the European countries. But now they wanted to portray themselves as the masters of Asia.

The Japanese, flushed from their coastal victories against the Chinese and seemingly intent on challenging the Western powers—particularly Britain and the United States—created incident after incident to prove to the Chinese, whose hatred of the 'island dwarfs' was conspicuous, that their white allies were no longer powerful enough to contain the might of Japan.

Militarily, the only force in the Pacific that could challenge Japan was that of the United States with its large fleet concentrated at Pearl Harbor in Hawaii and ancillary bases in the Philippines, Wake and Guam.

So Japan, condemned by the League of Nations, ran roughshod over China while the big Western powers stood fearfully by, insufficiently prepared for any test of strength.

With scant regard for the supposed neutrality of the International Settlement, the Japanese flooded their defense sector in the nearby Hongkew district with troops, warships on the river and massive armaments. Anti-aircraft emplacements were now visible throughout Hongkew.

Meanwhile, in America, the alarm felt by Great Britain and America over the course of events in Asia and the increasing hostility of the Japanese was expressed by President Roosevelt, who told Congress, 'Never before has American security been so seriously threatened.'

Shanghai suffered during the fighting between Japan and the Nationalists of China since Chinese airplanes did not hesitate to drop bombs on populated areas. On August 13, 1937, two small Chinese planes appeared over Shanghai, flying high to avoid the barrage of anti-aircraft fire unleashed by the Japanese in Hongkew.

The target of the planes appeared to be the ancient Japanese cruiser, *Idzumo*, permanently anchored close to Garden Bridge. It was a former Imperial Russian warship captured during the Russo-Japanese war of 1905. This was the headquarters of the Japanese Navy in Shanghai, impotent as a fighting unit but useful as a monument to commemorate the country's victory over a Western power.

The two Chinese planes maneuvered over the *Idzumo* but at such a height that accurate bombing was impossible. When the bombs were dropped they missed the ship completely. The bombs instead transformed two areas of the International Settlement into flaming infernos, in which more than one thousand people died.

The first bomb landed on Nanking Road between the Cathay and Palace Hotels. It created havoc. Hundreds of pedestrians of many nationalities became a whirling mass of burned victims. The trams were on fire. Motorists were incinerated in their blazing vehicles. Some who survived regretted that they did not die immediately; there were no facilities to care for such a large number, and they soon died in agony.

There was even greater devastation on Avenue Edward Seventh, where the second bomb dropped. This was the Chinese theater district, an area of street stalls, sideshows, shoppers and tourists. The carnage was appalling. Across the International Settlement, people could see plumes of smoke rising in the Chinese sectors.

The press coverage was so savage in condemning the Nationalists who were fighting the Japanese that all bombing raids by the Chinese on Shanghai were stopped. This was the last attack launched by the Chinese near the International Settlement area until the Americans entered the war in 1942.

Except for this horrific raid, the economic life of the International Shanghai was not particularly affected by the fighting because the port was still free and ships from all nations came and went without much difficulty. The Japanese in their turn did not interfere. They were, in fact, very interested in continuing Shanghai commercial and industrial activities with the outside world.

Just before World War II began in Europe, Hongkew, officially still part of the Settlement under the administration of the Shanghai Municipal Council, became a fully-controlled Japanese base.

The dreaded Japanese Kempetai (military police) imposed a reign of terror on the inhabitants there. The Japanese Consular Police took over street patrols in a direct challenge to the authority of the British-officered Shanghai Municipal Police. There were armed military and naval patrols on the streets and on Garden Bridge over the Soochow Creek, which was the boundary between Hongkew and the central area of the Settlement.

From time to time, the Kempetai would drag away Chinese men, screaming in fear, who had aroused suspicion. Their destination was the infamous Bridge House, close to the river.

Inevitably the foreign areas, more particularly the Settlement, were drawn into a test of strength between Japan and the treaty powers. In Nanking an anti-imperialist revolutionary and close friend of Dr. Sun Yat-sen by the name of Wang Ching-wei defected to the Japanese and agreed to create a new Chinese government. Wang, who ranked second only to Chiang Kai-shek in the Nationalist army, was installed by the Japanese as the head of 'The Reformed Government of the Republic of China.' Soon after, the Greater Shanghai government, a puppet administration known officially as the Ta Tao, established police stations challenging the control of the Shanghai Municipal Council controlled by the British.

The Ta Tao uniformed police watched the roads from the broad walls that protected the extensive grounds and mansions that housed various departments of the administration. The largest of the Ta Tao government administration buildings was on Jessfield Road. This Chinese-style residence consisted of several courtyards, cellars and a big garden that had been filled in with concrete to support two lines of barrack buildings.

The headquarters building struck fear into the hearts of the Chinese. Behind its high walls, following the Japanese pattern of brutality in other cities in China, anti-Japanese victims were subjected to diabolical forms of torture. Few of the men sent to the cellars for interrogation emerged alive.

This was still considered a war between Japan and Nationalist China. Despite the horrors committed against the Chinese, most Europeans did not feel the sting of the war in Shanghai until the Americans and British entered the Pacific theater in 1942.

George was typical of many in the International Settlements. He now was working in the Bund financial district near the port for an import export company while living in the Armenian Social Club building run by the Armenian Relief Society. He even helped direct various theatrical productions for the club.

George experienced little hardship during this period.

Chapter 7

"Fey Gee La La"

Some claim that the Japanese attacked the Americans in Hawaii because they felt invincible from their experiences during the occupation of China and elsewhere. The Japanese army had earned easy victories in Malaya, Singapore, the East Indies, and then—after the attack on Pearl Harbor—also in the Philippines, where the American military had moved from mainland China.

When the war with America started in late 1941, the Japanese immediately occupied the American and English consulates, took over all the banks, and entered the French Concession as well as securing the International Settlements. They were masters of Shanghai and were quick to prove it. The English police was demobilized, but the Japanese left a few of the Russian policemen because they needed a neutral party to maintain order.

Shortly after the attack on Pearl Harbor, a boat containing a high-ranking Japanese officer went upriver to demand the surrender of the British gunboat Petrel and the American gunboat, Wake. The Petrel had been instrumental in removing various missionaries from harm's way as the Japanese were advancing and fortifying their position along the China seacoast.

Now the British Petrel and the American gunboat, Wake, were the only two foreign naval vessels in the Whangpoo harbor. The Japanese officer demanded that both must surrender immediately.

After a brief skirmish, the Petrel was sunk in the harbor and the Wake surrendered. The captains and their crew were taken prisoner as they reached the Bund wharves.

The Japanese successfully boarded the Wake and, later in the morning, the Japanese naval ensign was flying from its stern as it made its way downriver over the large patch of oil that marked the watery graveyard of the Petrel.

The crews of the Wake and Petrel joined the British sailors and the American marines who had been left behind on guard duties at the Peking Legation and in Shanghai. A prison camp was set up on the Pootung side of the river in the heart of the countryside, where the prisoners were held for the duration of the war. This skirmish was the only battle of Shanghai.

Soon all British and American subjects who hadn't seized their opportunities to run away earlier were rounded up and interned in camps. All foreigners who were not part of the Axis alliance (Japan, Germany, Italy) or officially neutral were required to wear armbands. The British were issued red armbands printed with the letter 'B' and a number. The Americans wore armbands with an 'A,' the Netherlanders sported their individual numbers under the letter 'N,' and so forth. The armbands had to be worn whenever a foreigner went out.

Other than that, foreigners who were not British or American were not badly harassed. But soon everyone began to suffer economically because all the American and English firms were closed and their employees fired. The Japanese put their own citizens into the banks and other enterprises they took over, but these enterprises functioned poorly. The way the Japanese handled most economic matters was shortsighted and clumsy. They were constantly depleting resources for the war effort. Everything was appropriated. By the end of the war they had taken all the metal in the city, including statues and memorials.

When Shanghai first saw American airplanes, they were like a silver mass in the sky, enormous numbers of them, bombers together with fighter planes, flying over the city. People feared that the city was doomed. They remembered the carnage of the Chinese bombings in 1937. By the mid-1940s, the Japanese had built major fortifications. On every roof they tried to put some kind of anti-aircraft machine guns. They wanted to establish resistance everywhere.

All through the war and even earlier the Japanese in Shanghai were harassed by American bombers. The Flying Tigers under the command of General Claire Lee Chennault had operated as volunteers across Asia and conducted bombing raids against the enemy to keep the Burma Road from Rangoon to Chunking open. But initially Shanghai saw relatively little bombing. The Japanese had occupied most of the city, but it was not considered an industrial site by the Allies. Near the end of the war the biggest planes the Americans had were B-24s and B-29s. When those B-24s were flying overhead one would look up and see this huge silver object flashing in the sunlight. Although the Japanese had ordered anti-aircraft guns on all of the tall buildings, the guns couldn't reach the planes. The Japanese shot their guns, but the shells exploded halfway between the buildings and the plane.

After the bombing raids began on Shanghai, the Japanese employed Chinese they called Pall Chok. As soon as the Japanese would see any enemy planes they would send the Pall Chok out running through the streets with a bell. The Chinese runners would start yelling, *'Fey Gee La La, Fey Gee La La'*— 'planes are coming, planes are coming.' Those hearing the bell and warning cry would duck for cover. Since there were no bomb shelters, the Pall Chok would chase everyone into the doorways in case there was bombing in the streets.

In the end, the Americans kept the bombing of the city's center to a minimum. They would bomb the Chinese sector and the telephone companies and the power buildings. Aware of the internment camps around the city, they steered clear. However, many believe that Shanghai was destined to be destroyed by aerial bombardment, because surely anything that could conceivably support the war for Japan would have to be eliminated. If it hadn't been for the dropping of the atomic bomb and the quick Japanese surrender, the city would certainly have been extensively bombed.

When the Japanese emperor declared that he was willing to accept peace under any conditions, part of the Japanese military refused to believe that the surrender had taken place. However, when the armistice was finally declared, there was a tremendous amount of rejoicing and relief in Shanghai. The city had been spared.

Chapter 8

Shishka and His Gold

There were many fascinating characters who gathered at the Armenian Social Club in Shanghai during the war years. Some were people who came from Harbin; others escaped the Soviets after the Russian Revolution. Nearly 100,000 Russians crossed into Northern China in the ten years after the Revolution and before World War II. While some were successful merchants who moved into China from Irkutsk and Manzhouli to establish businesses in Harbin and Shanghai, others just barely got by. The Armenian immigrants always seemed to prosper. They were the ones who either ran or established businesses that would thrive even under Japanese occupation.

For example, one of the largest nightclubs that catered to Russians and Armenians in Shanghai was The Kavkaz. It was owned by a man named Mamikon Kardashian who was successful all through the war years. After the war ended, he catered to the American soldiers who briefly occupied Shanghai.

Another example was an import/export business run by Yervand Hamamdjian, who regularly traveled to Egypt for artifacts and was also the treasurer of the Armenian Social Club. Hamamdjian's father in law was a man named Assadurian with business interests in Shanghai and Manila in the Philippines. Assadurian controlled the Basque game of Jai Alai, a popular sports entertainment in Shanghai.

And then there was Shishka!

Shishka was one of the people George met at the social club during the Shanghai war years. George knew Shishka before the war in the late '30s in Harbin while he was visiting his family, and then in Shanghai at the club, but he knew little about Shishka's history.

His real name was known to be Garabed Ovanessian, but everybody called him Shishka or 'Garabed s shishkoy.' He did not seem to mind. He was known as a very jovial, gregarious fellow with a joke or a story for everyone. Most people did not know him well, but they all seemed to count him as an acquaintance. Perhaps it was his physical appearance that made him memorable and unusual.

He was called "Shishka" because of a lump on his neck—a gigantic red mole or wart on one side. As large as a goiter, it must have caused him discomfort. Shishka would tilt his head to one side, away from the sore, which made him look as if he was talking to people sideways. Because the growth was the size of a checker piece that one would use in backgammon (these checker pieces are called Shishki in Russian), people would call him Shishka. He was known by that name both in Harbin and Shanghai. He was often seen at church in Harbin or at the Armenian Social Club.

The growth on his neck was not Shishka's only peculiarity. Other idiosyncrasies also made him memorable. All year round he wore or carried a large fur coat whenever he went out. Fur coats for men were very fashionable in the late 1920s and '30s—full-length coats made of the finest fur with large collars. Most likely, he had purchased the coat for the cold sub-zero winters in Northern China then continued to wear it in Shanghai, even though the winters there were mild and the summers could get very hot. The coat was almost like a trademark; he was never without it. As a result he smelled (it wasn't clear whether the odor came from him or his coat), and very few could tolerate to be close to him for long. But he didn't seem to mind.

Shishka had a nice store in the center of the Harbin business district, which specialized in Brazilian coffee. It was called the Mocca Coffee Company and had branches in Shanghai. After customers bought the coffee, he would grind it according to their preferences. He also sold Swiss chocolates and candies. There were rumors that he imported other items inside the coffee, but no one had proof, and Shishka rarely talked about his business. Later George discovered that this peculiar man was the largest importer of coffee from Brazil. His businesses obviously afforded him a reasonable living, for he kept apartments in both Harbin and Shanghai and traveled back and forth often.

He wasn't particularly generous with his friends, but he was very fond of children. He would stuff small chocolates in his pockets and distribute them to children at church—but not until he'd squeezed and pinched their plump cheeks. At least that is what some of the children remember.

Another of Shishka's peculiarities was that he borrowed small amounts of money from everyone he knew. He was always begging his friends for small loans to tide him over a few days or a few weeks. Sometimes he would try to get money from the Armenian Relief Society, which was odd because the members of the Relief Society were usually the ones who solicited funds to continue the operation of the club. He was never gracious when paying back what he owed, and usually he would even pretend to forget and give the lender a hard time. After several bad experiences people would complain about him and avoid him. He didn't seem to mind. No one knew much more about Shishka, except that eventually he and George became reacquainted in Shanghai. And Shishka decided he needed a friend in Shanghai.

When they met again at the Armenian Social Club, Shishka and George had been acquainted for some years. This time Shishka unaccountably decided that George was a very close friend.

George did nothing specific to earn Shishka's friendship. However, each time Shishka saw George, he singled him out for a special embrace and told him how grateful he was to see his old friend. Initially George attributed this to Shishka's jovial nature and did not think much about it. Needless to say, with Shishka's hygiene problems these encounters were not all that welcome.

One particular day Shishka came to George at the social club tables and insisted that he accompany him to the bank.

"I need to get some of my money and I need you to help me," he said. George did not understand what he was really after, maybe another small loan.

"Why do you need me at the bank? Why not get the money yourself?" he asked.

"Well, you might have to help me with my money," was the only answer he received. George thought maybe he was afraid of going alone—Shanghai streets were well known for pickpockets and grab-and-run thieves—but surely he was not afraid of thieves during the day in the middle of the business district. Each major building in the business district had a huge Sikh guard in front, and the Sikhs were known to be particularly vicious with street thieves.

Perhaps Shishka needed someone to vouch for him. George was curious and decided to accompany him.

They met at the bank, where Shishka walked in with great confidence and made his presence known to all. Several of the clerks had risen from their desks the moment George and Shishka entered and came over to greet the strange man. They shook hands and smiled as if greeting an important official. Shishka insisted that he must see the bank president and the clerks assured him that the president had been informed of his arrival and would attend to him shortly. George stood beside Shishka and took in the show with confused amusement. Why were the bank people all making such a fuss over his friend, when he and everyone at the Armenian Club treated Shishka with mild indifference and sometimes even told jokes about him?

Suddenly the bank president appeared and with a warm handshake and broad smile hugged and greeted Shishka.

"What can I do for you, my good friend?" he asked.

"I need some of my money," answered Shishka. All the time glancing over at George to make sure George appreciated how well he was being treated.

"Of course, of course we will go into the vault immediately. I will help you personally," said the bank president. George wasn't sure he'd heard him correctly. Had he said the bank vault?

After Shishka introduced George as a friend who was going to help him with his money, they proceeded across the bank lobby as if this was all part of normal banking business. They all went through some heavy doors to the back. At the end of the hall, down some steps, there was the bank vault door covering the back wall. It was ajar during the day, and George, the bank president and two assistants walked in, led by Shishka, who looked as if he did this every day of the week.

The vault was lined with metal shelves and locked boxes. Several of the shelves had racks of money and on tables in the middle sat sacks that were full and sealed. George was very uncomfortable because he was certain that this whole business was not normal. After all, people were simply not allowed to walk in off the street and stroll into the bank vault, even with the permission of the bank officials. But the bank president and Shishka were in a very good humor.

In one corner of the vault, sitting on one of the shelves, was a pile of gold bars. These were not the large fifty-pound bars used in depositories to guarantee paper money. These were smaller bars about the size and shape of a thick credit card and weighing about two pounds each. They could be carried in a money belt if necessary.

George had only seen these types of bars at gambling houses and then very rarely. They were usually owned by people transporting gold from one region to another, or eccentrics who did not like to do business in paper money. The bars were all stamped to certify their purity and were stacked like poker chips on the shelf. This stack was the only gold visible in the vault, and it was of sufficient size to fill several deposit boxes if the bank had wanted them out of sight. Yet, there they sat in a corner of the vault. George noticed that one of the bank clerks was counting each bar as it was taken from the shelf and placed in a cloth bag.

He was obviously counting these against the known total, and there would undoubtedly be a fee for the withdrawal. Shishka took several small sacks and handed some to George to carry. There was thousands of dollars in gold in the small, heavy sacks.

George watched while Shishka exchanged some of the gold for paper credits. Then, after more laughs and handshakes, some papers were signed and they were out the door.

Outside the bank they boarded a mandarin rickshaw and began to move across town to Shishka's apartment. George now understood why Shishka needed help with his banking transactions; the gold in the sacks were heavy and cumbersome. After an awkward silence George began to question Shishka. "What was that all about in the bank," he asked? "Why did you bring me here?"

"I told you," Shishka answered, "you are my friend and I trust you to help me with my money."

"Don't talk rubbish," George said. "Why is all your money in gold in that vault? Why do you have your money in gold bars on a shelf? Why do they allow you to do this? Where did you get so much gold?"

Shishka laughed at each question. "I own a significant part of that bank," he answered. "They know me well there. The gold is my fortune and my family's. I don't trust Chinese paper script. With this war between the Japanese and the Chinese, paper is too volatile to suit me. I predict that soon there will be war with the British and maybe even the Americans. So, if I deal in European currency, it attracts the attention of the Japanese who are suspicious of people with large amounts of American or British money. Therefore, I have my money all in gold. Everyone accepts gold," Shishka explained with some emphasis.

"Actually," he continued, "I don't trust banks, either. But since I have a large interest in that bank, I made arrangements with the officials to hold my money in their vault and let me visit it regularly to withdraw what I need. Everything is handled very confidentially. They let me in the vault so I can see for myself everything is safe. Of course they charge me a handsome fee, but it is worth it to protect my fortune."

Apparently Shishka's family was wealthy and had migrated east during the Russian Revolution. Like so many wealthy Russians, they found it easier to send money and people east to Vladivostok and Harbin than to Europe. This was actually not uncommon in those days. George's father had also been given a large amount of gold by his family to create a business in China. Unfortunately, George's father had lost most of that gold gambling in Irkutsk.

As George talked to Shishka, the whole scene started to make sense, although George could think of many ways of handling the gold without the drama he had just witnessed. But George was sure that part of the reason for Shishka's show had been to impress his friend.

Still confused, George asked, "If you have all this gold in the bank and do not need money, why do you keep borrowing small amounts of money from your friends and acquaintances? Why do you ask the relief society for money you don't need? Have you no shame? "

"What are you talking about?" Shishka asked with some indifference.

"Well," George said as his temper began to rise, "I see you borrow small amounts from everyone you know and most often you give people trouble when they ask you to pay them back. Aren't you ashamed of yourself for being such a miser and a sponge with your friends? Aren't you ashamed of yourself for borrowing money you don't need?"

"Ashamed? Why should I be ashamed? Why should I care if people think I am cheap? It does not matter whether I need it. I borrow the money because it's a challenge," Shishka answered.

"A challenge, you mean like a game? Borrowing money is just a game for you? Isn't it embarrassing when people keep chasing after you, asking you to give back the money you borrowed?"

Shishka looked puzzled and shook his head. "Ashamed? Embarrassed? What is wrong with you, George? You don't seem to understand anything about money. Now look—why should I be ashamed? After all, I work very hard to borrow money from people. And I believe that people should work just as hard to get their money back."

"After all," he went on, "how we acquire and manage money is the greatest challenge in our lives in this modern world. And money is the only measure of value in our modern times."

George told this story many times as a lesson of life he learned from Shishka. He saw it as an example of how bizarre people are when it comes to money, how money can affect the way we behave toward each other, and how people among us are not always quite who they seem to be.

George assumed that this incident was just one of several withdrawals that Shishka made as war came to Shanghai, though he did not participate in many others. George found out that the withdrawals were all part of a detailed plan Shishka had concocted.

Because Shishka was anticipating the Japanese war with the Europeans, he was certain that the Japanese military would soon want an accounting of all the assets in the banks in Shanghai as well as any of the large businesses. His gold could be taken for the war effort.

So Shishka was carefully moving his gold into his Shanghai apartment and burying it behind a wall in the building. He felt that this way he could keep it hidden and safe.

In 1942, soon after that visit to the bank with George, World War II began in the Pacific and Shishka's worst fears came true. He had successfully moved his gold from the bank to the wall in his apartment, before the bank was seized by the military. Just as Shishka had predicted, during the course of the war, the Japanese seized everything valuable—commandeering all the business assets and even the metal from public statues for the war—but Shishka's fortune was safe.

He had dug a niche in the walls of his domicile and put the gold behind the walls. He covered the niche with plaster and paint, and disguised it so well that there did not appear to be anything unusual about the apartment.

After the Japanese had been defeated in 1945, the Americans came, and they also were very curious about the banks and businesses of Shanghai. They were particularly interested in any black market transactions using gold. So Shishka continued to keep his gold safely hidden. Three years later, Mao's guerrilla army drove out the Chinese Nationals and then the Americans began to leave Shanghai. But Shishka's gold was safe. He was still in Shanghai when the Chinese Communists took over the city in 1949.

Almost immediately the Communists began to dictate conditions to all business owners and residents. Most non-Chinese were not allowed to own homes in Shanghai because they were outrageously expensive. So everyone in the international community rented their home or apartment, and eviction was common. One day there was a knock on the door and Shishka faced a Communist Commissar and a squad of soldiers. He was told that his apartment house was being requisitioned by the military for use by soldiers that were stationed in the city. He was to pack his personal belongings and get out. The Commissar watched carefully as Shishka slowly packed and vacated his apartment.

Suddenly Shishka found himself out in the street, with no way to get to his gold. If he said anything or attempted a bribe, he risked retaliation for hoarding wealth. He still had his businesses, but travel had become more and more restricted under Communist control. He realized that he would have to abandon his gold.

The Communists added more restrictions. They wanted everything under Chinese control and disagreed with the old Japanese policy of letting the International Settlements run their own businesses and pay fees and taxes. Finally the Communists issued an order that any 'foreigners' could pay a fee and leave China because there would be no more work in Shanghai for them. If they stayed they ran the risk of being accused of spying for the Europeans. They had to go to any country that would accept them.

For the non-Chinese—no matter how long they had been in the Orient, even if they had been born there, and no matter what their political affiliations—the Communists made it impossible to conduct business under the new regime. Shishka decided to sell his business for whatever he could get and leave the Orient.

He never went back to claim his golden treasure and died in America more than a decade after leaving China.

Most of the opinions and observations about Shishka in this story are from transcripts of recorded conversations with George. In fact there are others who thought highly of this eccentric man. In Harbin he married a Russian lady but they did not have children, and no one knows what became of her. Among his businesses was a café and store called SANTOS, which sold Brazilian coffee and Swiss chocolates. He may have been a part owner in several other businesses as well as the bank where he kept his money. But no one knew for sure.

He was known to be in San Francisco in 1962 and by that time had removed the growth on his neck. He apparently still had some wealth. No one knows whether Shishka's gold was ever discovered back in Shanghai or what became of it. He never went back to claim it and died in America.

Chapter 9

The Conte Verde

The Whangpoo River
(Courtesy of Dr. Joseph Spinola)

War brings out the worst and the best in people. The tragedies, triumphs and chaos of war can test the character of people who might otherwise lead ordinary lives and go unnoticed. The circumstances surrounding the sinking of the Conte Verde serve as an example of the unsung heroes that come forward in war.

The Conte Verde was an ocean liner, a familiar sight to the residents of Shanghai. It had transported people from Europe to the Orient for many years. The destruction of the Conte Verde is a matter of historical record. Anyone can consult references and find details about the ship. But the story of how several Armenians helped the crew of this ocean liner was only told around the tables of the Armenian Social Club after the war ended.

In 1943, after the Italian Armistice, the Japanese wanted to grab the large Italian ship in the Shanghai Harbor. It was called the Conte Verde—Italian for "The Green Count." It originally provided transatlantic service between Genoa and New York. But after it became part of the Italian Trestina line that ran ocean liners between Asia and Europe, this ocean liner provided service between Trieste and Shanghai.

The Trestina fleet included the Conte Verde, Conte Rosso, and Conte Bianca, among others. They were similar to the American president ocean liners. At the time of the attack on Pearl Harbor in late 1941, the Conte Verde was caught in Shanghai and could not venture out of the harbor.

In the late 1930s, the Conte Verde and the Conte Rosso were used to carry large contingents of stateless Jews and immigrants to Shanghai. For many, it was the last bit of luxury between the hardships of Nazi Europe and the hardships that awaited them in the Orient. The use of these Italian ocean liners to move immigrants was a tale in itself.

The Nazis had taken over Germany and almost immediately began the persecution of Jews, Gypsies and Eastern Europeans. At first they actually encouraged the Jews to leave. But this became politically unattractive and they soon realized that putting them in camps was more efficient. Some Jews did petition to leave Germany and the Nazis loaded them on ships and sent them away without passports. The Nazis' intent was to demonstrate that the whole world was anti-Semitic. They were confident that no country would accept thousands of stateless Jews.

And, true to the times, these ships were denied entry at all ports of call, including the United States. During this period of worldwide depression, many countries had restrictive immigration policies. Most countries were also completely apathetic toward the Jews. And some were openly hostile and anti-Semitic.

If these ships could not find a port that would accept the immigrants, they were forced to go back to Germany, where all the undocumented undesirables would be put in concentration camps. However, when the Italian ocean liners arrived in Shanghai, the people were allowed to disembark because Shanghai was a free port and required no visas or passports. Soon word spread that the Conte Verde and the Conte Rosso could take people to safety in the Orient.

The Military Governor of Shanghai

The fact that the Conte Verde could disembark Jewish refugees in Shanghai upset the Nazi plan. An envoy—Gestapo chief and German representative to Japan, Joseph Meisinger—was sent on an official visit to convince the

Japanese military governor of Shanghai to refuse the immigrants' arrival, put them back on the ships and send them back to Germany.

In the late 1930s and all during the war years, Shanghai was under the direct occupation of the Japanese military. Even though there was a Chinese mayor of Shanghai, many diplomatic issues were brought before the military authority that controlled the city. The Germans bypassed the civilian authority and came to the military governor with their request about the Jews.

They even suggested to the governor that he could just drop the passengers overboard at sea or keep them prisoners and sail around until they starved to death. At this time the Japanese and the Germans were not allies, but it was obvious that the Germans, Japanese and Italians were sympathetic to one another politically and would eventually take sides against the British and French (and later the Americans) as World War II began to take shape. So the governor faced a delicate diplomatic situation.

The Japanese military governor called in the Jewish community leaders and, to gauge their reaction, told them what was demanded by the Germans. The Jewish leaders had already been warned what to expect and brought gifts and presented arguments to the governor to allow the refugees to stay in Shanghai.

Near the end of the meeting, the stern governor fell silent for a moment and finally asked, "But why do the Germans hate you so much?" One of the leaders was a rabbi named Reb Kalish who had been silent throughout most of the meeting because of language limitations. But he answered without hesitation in Hebrew, and his answer was immediately translated by an assistant, "They hate us because we are Oriental." (Some claim the translation was '*They hate us because we are short and different,*' but the effect was the same.)

The governor considered the answer for a moment and for the first time smiled. Despite any alliance with the Nazis, he decided to let the Jews stay. To appease the Germans, the Japanese authorities imposed additional business restrictions on the Jews. In 1942 they created a restricted ghetto in the northeast corner of Shanghai for the Jewish immigrants. It was called the Hongkew Ghetto.

From 1937 to 1943, Hongkew was the designated area for newly arrived stateless refugees. Thousands of Jews came to Shanghai fleeing Nazi persecution. The Japanese occupation authorities regarded them all as "stateless refugees" and set up this designated area to restrict their residences and business dealings. The designated area was bordered by Gongping, Tongbei, Huiming, and Zhoujiazui Road and carried warning signs in Chinese, Hebrew and English. Yet, despite the restrictions, the people in Hongkew regularly crossed the Garden Bridge and did business with the

The Conte Verde - 1943

(Postcard from "the sinking of the TSS Conte Verde" by Ralph Harpuder)

settlers in the International Settlement.

The governor was by no means the only Japanese official to help refugees trying to escape the Nazi Holocaust. One of the most famous was a Japanese diplomat named Chiune Sugihara, who was serving as Vice Consul for the Japanese Empire in Lithuania. He helped several thousand Jews leave the country of Lithuania by issuing transit visas to Jewish refugees so that they could travel to Japan. Most of the Jews who escaped were refugees from Poland or residents of Lithuania. In Japan many of these people stayed in Kobe, which to this day has a Jewish population and a synagogue.

When asked why he risked his career to save these people, Sugihara quoted an old Japanese saying, "Even a hunter cannot kill a bird which flies to him for refuge." Because of his actions in saving Jews from the Nazis, Sugihara was honored by Israel as Righteous among the Nations.

Ironically, there is no record that the Shanghai military governor received any recognition for his actions—this, despite evidence of the many refugees who were saved in Shanghai. This oversight is particularly egregious when you consider the numbers. With combined government and individual efforts, it is estimated that Shanghai sheltered some 24,000 Jewish refugees in the Hongkew ghetto during the war years. Some historians believe that the Japanese military governor of Shanghai saved more Jews from the Nazi Holocaust than all the Commonwealth countries combined.

There was never a tree planted, or a statue or a plaque in his name. After the war, he was simply forgotten. That is, by everyone except those who met at the social club. Whenever Armenians and Jews met at the club during and after the war, his heroism was always a topic of conversation. "Why was the governor who saved so many not given any recognition for his effort?", the patrons would ask one another.

And yet, for years after the war, in the Armenian Social Club, the governor general was not forgotten.

Yervand and the Italian Captain

Many refugees came to Shanghai on the Italian ocean liners of the Trestina line. This was how the Conte Verde happened to be trapped in Shanghai harbor when war broke out in 1942.

Then, one morning in 1943, the 19,000-ton luxury liner was found on its side sunk in the Whangpoo River near the Bund. It had been scuttled during the night, and no one seemed to know what had happened.

It was later learned that the ship was scuttled by its own Italian crew before the Japanese could take possession.

The Italian captain of the Conte Verde got stuck in the Shanghai Harbor after the 1943 Armistice but was determined to prevent the ship from being taken by the Japanese. The Japanese gendarmerie was looking for him because, instead of handing the ship over to the Japanese as agreed, he and members of his crew had sabotaged the ocean liner during the night.

The Messenger & Marrakeen Building where George was working for the Egyptian Trading Company was directly across from where the ship was lying in the harbor. He could look out the windows and see it there in the water of the Whangpoo River, lying on its side.

Yervand (Edward) Hamamdjian, George's employer at the time,

complained bitterly about the sinking of the ocean liner. As it turned out, he had traveled on the ship many times, and the Italian captain was well known to Yervand and well liked. George and his friend Leon worked in a building that faced on the Bund and they both worked for Yervand at the Egyptian Trading Company. They all knew each other from the Armenian Club and had become friends. Yervand was a regular visitor to the club since he was treasurer and a relative of the president.

And, in fact, Yervand became godfather to George's son in 1944.

Soon after the Conte Verde had been scuttled, strange things began to happen. Yervand began to ask George to buy extra food and bring it to his apartment. George was understandably confused, because Yervand had never asked for such favors before. The first few trips, Yervand or his wife, Alida, would take the groceries at the door, without inviting George into the apartment.

Initially Yervand would not explain why he wanted George to do the shopping in the marketplace for him. Later Yervand insisted that he did not want to attract any attention buying extra food because rationing was in place and the police were monitoring how much people were buying for their household. He did not want to be suspected of hoarding. Somehow this did not ring true. So the next time George came with the groceries, he refused to hand them over until he got an explanation. He stayed in the hall while they argued inside in quiet voices. Then they motioned for him to come in. When he entered the apartments, he immediately realized what Yervand had done.

Yervand knew the Conte Verde ship and crew well. Prior to the World War, his wife and her parents took this ship on regular trips whenever they'd go from Shanghai to Egypt on business. When George brought the extra food, he discovered that Yervand was hiding the captain and some crew members in his apartment.

Everyone knew that if the Kempeitai captured the captain and his crew, they would kill them or put them in an internment camp. Anyone harboring the captain and his crew would be treated no better.

If the situation was not so serious, it would be almost comical. The reason for the extra groceries was that the Italians were complaining about the Chinese food. Because some of the crew wanted a taste of home, George was required to buy Chinese pasta or noodles and some version of red sauce. Once he learned the truth, George would go regularly to the market and if anyone should ask, he would tell them that his new wife was experimenting with a new chop suey recipe or learning to cook Italian. Although all the recipes looked suspiciously like spaghetti and meat sauce, no one seemed suspicious.

Shortly after the Conte Verde had been scuttled, the Japanese decided that they would re-float the ship. So they took gargantuan chains from the ship and anchored them round the building where George was working. They started to tow the ship closer to the shore, and when they had brought it close enough, they filled it full of air and lifted it to the surface. This was a huge passenger ship, and the Japanese believed that they could use it as an Army troop transport. As soon as it was afloat, the Japanese made plans to move it from Shanghai to Kyoto, refit it and use it to move aircraft equipment and troops.

People in the Armenian Club had mixed feelings about the whole operation. Some were sympathetic to the idea of recovering the ship. After all, this was one of the ships that had brought so many refugees from Europe. It symbolized the last bit of European luxury. The Jewish refugees in particular who came on the Conte Verde were now restricted to a miserable ghetto and the Conte Verde was a wonderful reminder of escape, good fortune and hope. It seemed a shame not to recover it.

Others argued that the ship must not be used by the Japanese to further their war effort. The Conte Verde was no longer a luxury ocean liner but a war prize that would be converted into a troop and armament carrier. It should stay in the harbor or be destroyed as the Italian crew had originally planned.

George was actually happy to see the ocean liner leave the Shanghai Harbor. As long as it was disabled in the Whangpoo River, it was no problem but once it was raised, the ship made a tempting target for the Americans. Bombing raids in Shanghai were rare and usually restricted to the other side of the Garden Bridge away from the International Settlements.

But if a squadron of bombers were sent to destroy the Conte Verde before it could be moved down the Yangtze, the entire harbor could become a target. It would be like the earlier bombings of Shanghai by the Nationalists. Since George worked near the harbor, this threat caused him a great deal of anxiety.

As it turned out, as soon as the ship left the Whangpoo and was barged on the Yangtze River, the Americans were waiting. Lt. General Claire Lee Chennault, commanding officer of the China-based 14th US Air Force, made the decision to sink the ocean liner before the Japanese could use her for their military effort. Aerial reconnaissance showed that preparations were finished by the Japanese, and they were ready to move the ship by the middle of 1944.

Details of the military action against the Conte Verde were provided in an interview with Colonel William D. Hopson, who led the raid. There were two alternatives for attacking her, either by daylight—bombing from high altitude using several bombers with fighter escort—or by night—attacking with a single plane at a low altitude and making a quick getaway. It was decided that a single plane was the best alternative to minimize civilian casualties, and Colonel Hopson of the 308th bombardment group took charge of the preparation and execution of this mission.

A B-24 bomber was selected and fitted with special sights and torpedo bombs. Early in the morning on August 8, 1944, Colonel Hopson and his crew flew a low-level bombing raid along the Yangtze. They struck the Conte Verde as it was being moved down the Yangtze River on its way to Japan and it was sunk. Another attempt at salvage also ended in a successful bombing raid and the Japanese finally abandoned any further efforts. That was the end of the Conte Verde.

The captain and several others stayed hidden in their friend's apartment for more than a year, until the end of the war. George met the captain many times and remembered him as a short guy with a chubby face. The captain's name was Signore Di Bei or something similar. In addition, there were two other crew members staying at the residence for the duration along with the captain. One of them was remembered as Rosario. When the war was over, they joined in the victory celebration.

After the war, the crew of the Conte Verde was honored by the American military for its wartime resistance. But the ship was quickly forgotten, despite its service in saving countless lives transporting undocumented immigrants to the free port of Shanghai.

The actions taken to protect the crew constituted genuine heroism. People engaged in sabotage and harboring an enemy in time of war were subject to harsh treatment and even execution. Yervand was an unsung hero, who had provided help to his friends at a critical time in the midst of chaos.

George's friend Yervand had Egyptian citizenship and left China in 1948. His family is now far flung, but his son supplied additional information. In 1955, Yervand Hamamdjian changed his name to Edward Gerard for reasons of business and moved to Los Angeles, California. He retired after forty years running various businesses in California and died in 2004. He is survived by his son and daughter, Edwin and Michele, who live in Tunisia and America respectively. His wife Alida also lives in California.

Nothing more is known about the captain or crew of the Conte Verde. It is presumed that they were repatriated to Italy after the war.

Chapter 10

Adventures with the Clergy

George's father died in Harbin in 1933, when George was twenty-one. Until he finally decided to move to Shanghai in 1937, George wandered around Asia. That was where he first met Rev. Fr. Assoghig Ghazarian. Understanding their relationship (beyond just parishioner and priest) requires some background.

The church in Harbin was the largest Armenian house of worship in Northern China; only the Far-Eastern Armenian Apostolic in Vladivostok on the Eastern border of Russia was larger. After the Russian Revolution, the priest in Vladivostok, Fr. Yeghishe Rostomiants, moved to Harbin and became the spiritual leader for all Armenians in Manchuria, China and Japan. The Armenian colony that had been part of Harbin since the beginning of the twentieth century was quite extensive. In the mid-'30s there were about 400 parishioners in the Armeno-Grigorian Church of Harbin. The church was built in 1923 and registered in 1925 in memory of St. Gregory the Illuminator. Fr. Yeghishe Rostomiants, who served there for fifteen years, died in 1932. For several years the church was without a pastor, and during that time it was rented to members of the Anglican Congregation in the city.

In 1937, thanks to the efforts of prominent citizens and the Armenian National Organization, a priest was brought to Harbin from Jerusalem. This was the Rev. Fr. Assoghig Ghazarian. Officially Rev. Fr. Assoghig was a British citizen and not a displaced Armenian. He was a citizen of Jerusalem, which at that time was a British protectorate.

Rev. Fr. Assoghig's parents were killed by the Turks when he was a child at the end of World War I, and he was sent to a monastery for care. Well educated in the monastery, he decided to join the priesthood. He was very erudite and spoke several languages.

At the time he took over the Harbin church in 1937, he was twenty-seven years old. People who knew him then described him as a handsome, dark and intense young man with heavy Armenian eyebrows who did not tolerate any nonsense or disrespect from his flock. When George first met the priest, he was twenty-five years old and just becoming familiar with life in Shanghai.

After he was given responsibility for the faithful in Shanghai, Fr. Assoghig would come regularly to Shanghai from Harbin, where his normal parish was located. He had made arrangements with the Bishop Victor of the Russian Orthodox Church in Shanghai to use a corner of their recently built cathedral called the Saint Nicholas Orthodox Greek Catholic Cathedral on Route Doumer to display the Armenian icons and allow Armenian parishioners to worship on special religious holidays. Most of the time services were held on Sunday at the Armenian Social Club. That was where Fr. Assoghig met George.

Unfortunately, the priest did not speak or understand Russian, and the Bishop of the Russian Orthodox Church did not speak English. But Fr. Assoghig discovered that George knew both English and Russian, so when he needed help with the Russian bishop, he would insist that George accompany him.

This was how the priest, Assoghig and George came to see each other regularly. At roughly the same age, they had some interests in common, but the priest would never let George forget that he was a priest and should be respected. He would regularly use his shepherd's staff for emphasis. There was one incident early in their relationship that George remembered in particular. It happened at the Armenian Club.

One day the priest was at the Armenian Club to greet the people there and encourage them to attend services on Sunday. George had introduced him to the people he knew and answered questions if there were any problems.

Noticing the billiard table, Fr. Assoghig said, "Let's play," and asked George to show him how to play pocket billiards.

George showed him how to hold and use the cue stick, line up the ball with the pocket, and the best way to hit the ball. Very quickly the priest became more and more competent. Every time he hit the ball and the ball would fall in the pocket, he would stand back and say *"Ho, Ho, Ho"* and point as if to emphasize his new skill.

George thought that was pretty funny. Soon after, every time George hit the ball into the pocket, he would stand back and say *"Ho, Ho, Ho"* as well.

Suddenly Fr. Assoghig took the pool cue and started hitting George on the head. George backed up and said to him, "Why are you hitting me?"

The priest said, "Why are you laughing like that?"

George told him, "Well, you are laughing, too, every time you hit the ball in the pocket."

"Yes," he said, shaking his finger at the young man, "but I am Vartaped (a priest of higher education). You are not Vartaped."

So there was George, not really a deacon of the church or any other official position, more like a personal helper to the priest. He was regularly selling candy and collecting money for the church by passing the plate each Sunday during services at the club. Every so often he would go with the priest to visit the Russian Bishop and arrange for a special religious ceremony.

Incidentally, this Russian bishop was a former officer in the White Army who had joined the church late in life. After he became a monk he would wrap himself in chains as a penance; with chains all over his body, he would tighten them until he bled. He was, incongruously, 'a filthy guy, dirty like you wouldn't believe' (according to George).

So, every time the Rev. Fr. Assoghig would come from Harbin he would visit the Russian Bishop.

Because the Armenians didn't have a church in Shanghai, the Bishop allowed the icons of St. Gregory to hang in the cathedral. The arrangement was that if the Armenians wanted to go and pray, they could go to the cathedral and worship before the icons. This was a huge cathedral, and the Bishop lived in quarters provided at the cathedral. Of course, whenever Fr. Assoghig and the Bishop would meet they would hug and kiss each other and George was expected to do the same.

Each meeting was formal and respectful, but because of these meetings with the bishop, everyone but George was allowed to take Communion on Sunday.

Without explaining his reasoning, Fr. Assoghig had decided that George must take his Communion on Saturday and fast with him all Saturday and Sunday. For the priest, fasting didn't just mean not eating—George didn't mind that—for him, fasting meant abstaining from drinking as well. He didn't let George drink a drop of water all day long on Saturday, and services were in the evening for Communion. So after not drinking all day, George would also have to endure the evening services with no water. When the services ended, he would go to the faucet and drink like a horse.

One Saturday the Russian Bishop decided to pay a surprise visit to the Armenian Club on the day before Easter Sunday. As host for the Easter service, Fr. Assoghig was busy making unleavened bread. When the Chinese assistant who was working there told him that the Bishop had come to visit, the priest picked up his robe and ran upstairs to get cleaned up, telling George on the way that he would need his help to translate. When Fr. Assoghig came down again, he turned to the Chinese assistant to order Turkish coffee for the Bishop.

The Chinese assistant brought Turkish coffee served with a glass of water for the Bishop and his assistant—also for the priest and George.

George sat quietly for a few minutes and then decided, 'I'm going to drink that glass of water because I'm dying of thirst.' He figured out that the priest was not going to say anything in front of the Bishop. So there was the water and coffee in front of George and the water and coffee in front of the priest … The Bishop and his assistant were drinking coffee and talking to the priest, but the priest did not touch anything because he was fasting. George waited until he believed the priest was distracted by the conversation and casually extended his hand to take the glass of water.

Immediately Fr. Assoghig (in Armenian) told him with a stern look: 'Che!' (Not allowed.)

A few minutes later the Chinese helper took away everyone's coffee and water. George had to sit there 'feeling like a dummy' and continuing to suffer.

This was George's life with the clergy.

However, George and his friend Leon occasionally enjoyed playing tricks on the young priest.

Leon and George enjoyed each other's company for many years. They were co-workers at the Egyptian Trading Company on the Bund.

Leon was something of a practical joker. In fact, each time the priest would come to Shanghai, Leon would try to play a joke on him. Sometimes he would call Fr. Assoghig's assistant and pretend to be someone of great importance; then he'd try to see how long he could keep the deacon or the priest on the telephone before the hoax was uncovered. Other times he would invite the priest to an important affair that did not exist. He was careful to avoid Assoghig's shepherd's staff, because the priest began to suspect who was making these crank calls and coming up with these tricks, and looked for Leon or George whenever things were going mysteriously awry. These practical jokes were not reserved for the priest alone. Leon and George were always trying to pull a fast one on someone. They just had the most fun with the priest.

The best joke of all involved a lady who was very impressed with the young priest.

The Lady and the Toilet Cushion

It was mentioned earlier that the priest was quite good-looking and highly regarded by everyone because he had come all the way from Jerusalem to take care of the parishioners here in China. What wasn't clear was whether he would marry. Priests of the Armenian Church can marry either by contract or at the time they become priests. *Der Hayr* is a married priest and *Hayr Soorp* is a celibate priest. In addition, there was a class of scholars of higher education addressed as *Vartapeds*.

Fr. Assoghig was well known in Harbin. The Russian newspapers had announced his arrival from Jerusalem. Very quickly Armenians and even faithful Russians who met him on the street would treat him with great respect and call him Vartaped. But because this priest was new to the Shanghai congregation and past priests had married and raised families, there was still some confusion. He came to Shanghai infrequently, and when he was available for services at the Armenian Club, his presence was still a novelty.

Both Leon and George knew well that Fr. Assoghig was a monk and Hayr Soorp, and that he had decided to continue his studies within the Armenian Church.

In fact, later in life, he would rise in the ranks of the church. But at this time he was still new in Shanghai. Some of the ladies were very interested in the priest but did not dare address personal subjects because they were daunted by his stern demeanor. However, one of the ladies was so taken with Assoghig that she sought out more information.

If she had talked to others in the congregation, the entire incident might never have happened. Unfortunately she made the mistake of approaching the two who were the least reliable. Having noticed that Leon and George were both on good terms with the priest, she asked whether they could suggest a gift for him. She hoped to present it the next time he was available in Shanghai. She told the men that she was very good with a needle and would like to make a personalized gift, like a scarf or a shawl or even an embroidered pillow. She asked George what would be appropriate. This was a big mistake.

The question may seem innocent enough, but it presented too tempting an opportunity for the two scoundrels, who could not resist. They immediately began to explore the possibilities of an *appropriate* gift from the young lady.

George carefully explained to her how Fr. Assoghig would share with him a complaint about the cold mornings in Harbin. It seemed the priest could put up with anything but a cold toilet seat, which was just so uncomfortable on a frigid morning.

Eventually they were able to persuade the young lady that what he needed was something special for those cold mornings. What he needed, what would be perfect, and what would be appreciated more than anything else, was an embroidered pillow shaped into a toilet seat cushion. The lady may have been understandably skeptical, but she was sufficiently gullible and trusting. George and Leon assured her that this would be the ideal gift, and truly welcome. The lady was young and, to their credit, the two were very persuasive as they

Father Ghazarian (with cross) and clergy

weaved and embellished the story of the priest's discomfort.

Fr. Assoghig was in Harbin while George coached this woman in Shanghai on what would be an appropriate gift. It took some time, but finally she agreed.

The next time the priest came to Shanghai, after the services at the social club had concluded, the lady came forward and presented a wrapped gift to Fr. Assoghig. George made certain to be out of sight when the priest graciously accepted the gift.

As soon as he opened it and realized what it was, he started to yell and chase the poor woman around the club, waving his shepherd's staff.

The poor woman ran off in tears; George never did find out what became of her. He also was never entirely certain whether Fr. Assoghig ever determined who was really behind this obvious breach of propriety. If there had been time for such personal matters, it would surely have all come out. But personal matters were soon pushed aside by declarations of war.

Within days of the toilet cushion incident, World War II broke out along the China coast and the trips between Harbin and Shanghai stopped. George lost track of Fr. Assoghig and only later was told what happened to him in Harbin.

During World War II, Rt. Rev. Fr. Assoghig Ghazarian was imprisoned in a concentration camp for British and American citizens in the city of Moukden. As soon as war was declared, he had been arrested, because his papers showed he had come from Jerusalem, a British protectorate. All British citizens were suspect as spies. He spent the entire war in the camp and was reported to have been badly treated by the Japanese.

After the war, Fr. Assoghig returned to Harbin but as the Communists took over China, more and more of the Armenian colony left. In 1950 he returned to Jerusalem, and the Armenian Church in Harbin became the property of the Chinese Government. It was eventually destroyed.

Many years later, the author had the privilege and pleasure to meet Rt. Rev. Assoghig Ghazarian. He was already an Archbishop of the Armenian Apostolic Church. In 1974, the author was living in Southern California, with his parents nearby. As Archbishop, the Rt. Rev. Assoghig had served in Los Angeles, Australia, Syria and Etchmiadzin in Armenia. The Archbishop was on a tour of the Western Dioceses in America and, at this time, was visiting California, which has a very large Armenian population. Rather than meet many of his congregation in a church, he arranged for them to greet him at a famous Los Angeles restaurant called The Kavkaz. The owner of the restaurant, Yervand Markarian, his talented wife Nunia and many of the patrons were refugees from Harbin and Shanghai who had lived in the Orient during the Pacific war and were now citizens of America. The Archbishop would be greeting people from his congregation he had not seen in thirty years.

My mother asked me to accompany her to the restaurant because she had known him when she was a young woman in Harbin. My father did not choose to join us.

He said he wasn't feeling well, or maybe he didn't want the old memories or was feuding with someone at the reception or someone from his Shanghai days (Armenians are always feuding with someone). Or maybe he just was not eager to face the Archbishop. At the time he didn't share his reasons.

There was a long reception line that extended to the back of the restaurant, and the Archbishop took time to say hello and share memories with each of the people who came forward to meet him. When it was my mother's turn, she stepped forward, and I could hear her asking the Archbishop whether he remembered her. They spoke for a few minutes and exchanged memories, and then she turned and introduced me as her son. The Archbishop looked at me for a moment as we exchanged pleasantries and then he leaned forward and said, as much as asked, "You are George's son?" When I nodded, he lightly cuffed me on the cheek in a pretend slap and said, "Say hello to your father for me," all the while shaking his finger disapprovingly. At the time, I had no idea what this was all about. It was only years later that I understood, having heard the whole story when my father was sharing his memories of Shanghai.

Almost ten years later my father confessed. When he told me the stories of his encounter with the cleric, I remembered the slap and thought that perhaps some of the sins of the father are visited on the son after all.

Chapter 11

Varak and the Brilliant Spy

In 1932 an undeclared war between Japan and China was making life difficult for most of the civilians. The Kempeitai were in a state of heightened alert and rumors were flying that a Russian spy was operating in Harbin and Shanghai. He was suspected of spying for the Soviets, and it was thought that his name was Vladimir Sergeyev. Because of the similarity in names, George's brother Varak was mistakenly arrested. The Kempeitai insisted that the Russians explain who he was. He was taken to a place called Pagranechnaya. Since he had been identified as a spy and the Russians did not know anything about him, he was thrown into prison and beaten, even though he insisted he was innocent.

Varak kept arguing that they had the wrong man, that his name was Varak (Vladimir) Sergeeff, not Sergeyev, and that he had lived in Harbin for many years. His denials only angered the authorities and elicited regular beatings with bamboo rods. The prison guards simply told him that no mistake had been made.

Eventually the authorities determined that the real spy was an older man and Varak's true identity was established back in Harbin. The identity problem was cleared up but not before Varak had spent three grueling months in prison. When he was released, they told him to keep his mouth shut and allowed him to return to Harbin. This would have been the end of the sad incident, except that after a little investigating and with the help of rumors, it was discovered that Varak may have been mistaken for the most brilliant spy in modern history—perhaps the greatest spy of them all.

The Kempeitai were looking for someone who had practically the same name and was working for the Russians. They had grabbed Varak because of the similarity in names—his name was Sergeeff and the spy was Richard Sorge (also sometimes known as Sergeyev).

What was ironic about the name mix-up was that the original family name was Sarkesian, not Sergeeff at all. Varak took the name Vladimir Sergeeff because of a mistake made by his father when a census was taken in Baku before World War I. But when he had tried to explain that to the Kempeitai it only led to more beatings.

It seems that when the family was living in Russia-occupied Baku, Varak's father Levon was recruited by the czarist Russian armed forces along with all able bodied men. There was a census taken to register all males for possible service in the armed forces. The family name was Sarkesian. So when Levon reported for the census to register for the armed forces, they asked him "What's your name?"

He said, "Levon Sarkesian."

The Russian recruiter, who was not familiar with Armenian etymology, kept saying "Sarkes? Sarkes? What is this Sarkes?"

So, Levon said, "Oh, well, in translation Sarkes will be Sergei."

"Oh," said the recruiter, "then we will call you Sergeeff (son of Sergei)." And that was how the name Sergeeff was established. The family carried that name when they immigrated to Siberia and later to Northern China because it was easier to travel in Russia with a Russian name.

Varak, the older son, carried the name, Vladimir Sergeeff, with him from that time on. When he tried to explain the name mix-up, the authorities simply chose to believe that he was using an alias.

The real spy Sorge (rhymes with morgue) was born in Baku, and Varak Sergeeff was born in Baku. Sorge was born in 1895, while Varak was born in 1905, so they were close in age (Sorge looked younger than his years until he started drinking heavily). Varak regularly traveled between Harbin and Shanghai. It was rumored that Sorge had organized a spy ring in Harbin and Shanghai. Varak also physically looked like the spy Sorge. No wonder he was picked up and imprisoned.

Unfortunately, this was not the Sergeeff boys' first run-in with the Kempeitai. Several years earlier George had gotten into trouble when the military police thought he had an illegal shortwave radio. Simply telling them that they had made a mistake did no good and invited more attention. George was concerned that if he insisted on a fair review for Varak, his own run-in with the Kempeitai would come up again.

Established in 1881, the Kempeitai was patterned after the French Gendarmerie. However after 1930 they were more closely aligned in philosophy and tactics with the Nazi SS. They maintained public order in Japan under the direction of the Interior Ministry and had similar duties in occupied territories, but under the direction of the War Ministry. In the occupied territories the Kempeitai discharged the functions of secret police and could arrest without warrants those who were regarded as subversive or seditious.

The Kempeitai did not hesitate to use torture to extract forced confessions. By the end of World War II, there were over 36,000 regular members. George knew they had no sympathy or understanding. Everyone was under suspicion of being a spy. It was safe to say no one wanted to attract their attention.

The Shortwave Radio Raid

When George tried to intervene on his brother's behalf, his family was concerned that all the old troubles he had with the Kempeitai would resurface. As a young man in Dairen, George worked for the RCA Victor Company, which had a branch in Dairen. At RCA Victor, the employees were allowed to take radio receivers to their houses for private use. And George had one. The shortwave radio allowed you to listen to broadcasts in places like Shanghai and Hong Kong. They were prohibited because they allowed you to listen to news that was not controlled by the Japanese authority.

For example, the Americans were broadcasting news that was detrimental to the Japanese cause—news the Japanese didn't want the people living under Japanese occupation to hear.

Somehow the Japanese found out about George's shortwave radio, and the Kempeitai came to the house and turned it upside down. Apparently this was standard Japanese military police procedure. They were looking not just for a radio but for a transmitter. Someone had given them false information, claiming that George had a transmitter and was transmitting messages.

George knew one of the Kempeitai who had come to the house with the search party. George and the officer often gambled and drank together at the casino hotels, and George considered him a friend.

So he said to the officer, "You know me, you know who I am. Why don't you talk, why don't you say something to help me?"

But the officer said to George, "I don't know you, I never saw you, I don't know who you are."

After the search was over and the house was in shambles, they ordered George to cut the shortwave off the radio; which he did. They came back once again and checked to make sure that it'd been cut.

Several days later George met this acquaintance or friend from the Kempeitai at the main foyer room at the Rialto Hotel. When he saw George he was already half drunk.

He came over, hugged George and said, "George San ... this and George

San ... that, I'm so happy to see you, my good friend."

So George tried to control himself and asked, "What do you mean, 'good friend'? Do you remember that incident when you came to my house and denied you even knew me? Why couldn't you speak then? Why couldn't you call me your friend then?"

The officer sobered quickly and said, "George San, when the Japanese join the Kempeitai, they don't know nobody, they don't have family—no father, no mother—they don't have friends, nobody. That's the official policy. That's what they expect. I am sorry I could not help you but that is the policy. You must understand."

George looked at the officer and answered solemnly, "If you don't have family, you don't have anything." And he walked away.

After that incident George had very little use for the Japanese. He never could trust another one again. This prejudice, formed that day, stayed with him the rest of his life.

It was because of this earlier incident that George was so concerned for his brother. The Kempeitai simply did not admit mistakes. For three months, his brother was missing. It was a relief when news came that Varak had been released. As soon as he was released, he made his way back to Harbin and told the family the story about the mix-up. George began to think seriously about changing his name. It was dangerous to be a Sergeeff while this spy was still operating in the Orient.

Chapter 12

The Spy Sorge

The spy Sorge who was working for Stalin before and during World War II was perhaps "the most formidable spy in history."

This was the opinion of Ian Fleming, the creator of James Bond. He was called "brilliant" by Tom Clancey, and "the spy to end spies" by John Le Carré. Sorge's exalted reputation was little consolation to Varak and did not make the pain he'd suffered at the hands of the Kempeitai easier to bear, but if he'd had to be misidentified as a spy, it may as well be the best spy in history.

Sorge was born in Baku in 1895 to a Russian mother and a German father, a mining engineer. He served with distinction in World War I but became a strict Marxist in his twenties and began serving the Fourth Bureau in Soviet Russia in 1930. He was sent to Shanghai in 1930 to help initiate a Communist revolution in China. He gathered intelligence about the Chinese leader Chiang Kai-shek and his supporters. Posing as an agricultural researcher, he was able to travel throughout China, working with underground Communist groups and gathering information.

In the late 1930s, he posed as a news correspondent and was put in contact with the Japanese journalist Hotsumi Ozaki, from whom Sorge would receive intelligence information for several years about the Japanese. He even got information that the Japanese were planning an attack on the Hawaiian Islands. The information was sufficiently precise that Sorge reported an attack on America scheduled for late 1941.

Sorge also worked with a friend of Ozaki's named Teikichi, a correspondent for the *Shanghai Weekly*.

As hostilities between Japan and China escalated, Sorge reported back to Moscow about the readiness of Chinese troops and their chances against a

Richard Sorge

(Bundesarchiv Bild 183-1985-1003-020)

superior Japanese military. After Ozaki returned to Japan, Sorge fell under suspicion of being a spy. He was wrongly identified as likely being an agent for Germany. To enhance his cover as a journalist, he wrote complimentary articles about members of Chang Kai-shek's military circle, who conferred with Sorge, thus unknowingly providing him with bits of valuable information. He had operated a successful spy ring for nearly ten years before the Japanese began to get suspicious.

In fact everyone was becoming suspicious. In keeping with the oppressive police state the Japanese were running, the Kempeitai would on occasion round up Communist sympathizers and persons of interest.

It was during one of these sweeps that George's brother Varak was arrested and mistaken for a spy. And it was because of these sweeps that Sorge was recalled to Moscow and reassigned. He was sent to Japan to spy on the Japanese directly in the homeland. While the Kempeitai were looking for Sorge in China, he was actually in their backyard.

It was because of his excellent work in China that Sorge was dispatched to Japan. His Soviet superiors felt that he might be the only agent who could obtain intelligence information in Japan, which was at that time extremely secure against leaks. Japan had become a police state in the true sense of the word, and security was very tight. All foreigners were subjected to continual scrutiny by its fervent authorities and the Kempeitai.

The Russians saw the brutal Japanese conquests of Manchuria at the beginning of the 1930s as a prelude to further expansion into Russian Siberia. The German and Japanese treaties of 1936 seemed to confirm this belief. Sorge was assigned to determine whether Japan was prepared to move militarily against China, with a primary goal of investigating the feasibility of developing a Soviet spy network in Japan.

On arrival in Japan, Sorge struck up a friendship with a German named Eugen Ott, who later became an ambassador. It is possible that Sorge was a double agent, for he did give information to Ott. It was also rumored that Sorge seduced the ambassador's wife.

Sorge was an enormous favorite of the fairer sex; the Tokyo police later found at least twenty girls who claimed to have had affairs with him. He was very keen on drinking to all hours of the night, night after night, and yet could still rise early to do his job without a care.

In September 1939, when war broke out in Europe, Sorge was head of an efficient intelligence group. Information was sent to Siberia from a transmitter and later dispatched to Moscow. He provided three valuable pieces of information that could have changed the course of history. He was able to determine that the Nazis were planning an invasion of Russia in early 1941 and even pinpointed the date of the invasion. Unfortunately Stalin dismissed the reports. He simply could not believe that Hitler would betray him and break the non-aggression treaty the two dictators had signed. Stalin was also paranoid about information from spies. Operation Barbarossa went off on schedule and Germany invaded Russia on June 22, 1941, just as Sorge had foretold. Stalin became severely depressed after the invasion and Hitler was able to advance through the Ukraine and deep into Russia to Moscow and Stalingrad before the Red Army could stop him.

Postage Stamp

(In public domain of Russian Federation)

Sorge was also able to determine that the Japanese did not have any plans to invade Siberia (this information was believed and fourteen rifle divisions were moved from Siberia to help in the battle of Moscow in autumn 1941).

He was also able to instill mistrust in the Japanese of the German reliability as an ally during World War II.

During a routine sweep when the Kempeitai were looking for Communists, evidence surfaced that Sorge was indeed a master spy. He was captured in 1942. He was executed in 1944 in Sugamo Prison and buried in Japan.

Several years later, Leopold Trepper, head of the Red Orchestra, recalled a conversation with General Tominaga, who was Japan's Vice-Minister of Defense during WWII:

> "Why was Sorge sentenced to death in 1942 but not executed until November 7, 1944? Why didn't you propose that he be exchanged? Japan and the USSR were not at war."
>
> General Tominaga cut me off energetically. "Three times we proposed to the Soviet Embassy in Tokyo that Sorge be exchanged for Japanese prisoners. Three times we got the same answer: " 'The man called Richard Sorge is unknown to us.'
>
> Unknown—Richard Sorge? This man who had warned Russia of the German attack, and who had announced in the middle of the battle of Moscow that Japan would not attack the Soviet Union, thus enabling the Soviet chiefs of staff to bring fresh divisions from Siberia? They preferred to let Richard Sorge be executed rather than have a witness on their hands after the war that Stalin had been warned about the Nazis invasion and did not listen.

And yet, for some time after the war, there were rumors that the Japanese had secretly turned Sorge over to the Soviets in exchange for concessions in Manchuria. He was reportedly seen in Shanghai in 1947.

Finally in 1964 the Russians recognized Sorge, making him a Hero of the Soviet Union and issuing a stamp to commemorate his service to Russia. He may very well be the only real life spy with his own postage stamp.

Now, there is no concrete evidence that Sorge was the spy that the Kempeitai were looking for when they arrested George's brother Varak. But Sorge was operating in China from 1930 to the start of World War II, and the similarity between the two men was uncanny.

When George heard the story of what had happened to his brother because of the confusion over the family name, he decided it was time to change his family name.

He had always thought that it was silly to have a Russian name when he was actually Armenian, but his brother's bad experience provided extra impetus. Sometime after the war, when George was in Shanghai, he decided to drop the Russian name and change it to Sergoyan, which sounded more Armenian than Sergeeff. And that's how his family became Sergoyan, while his brother's remained Sergeeff.

The big puzzle here was why George did not go back to the original family name, Sarkesian. He was never able to explain why he decided on Sergoyan. Perhaps he still bore some resentment over his dad's gambling and those hard years in Harbin. Though this name translates into "son of Serge" with an Armenian ending, he simply remarked that it sounded more American to him, and by the end of World War II he had become very fond of the Americans.

Chapter 13

Nadia

In 1940, at the Armenian Social Club in Shanghai, George saw Nadia for the first time. He later commented that he first noticed a slender girl wearing a silly hat, but his friends were sure it wasn't the "hat" that caught his attention.

She was twenty-two years old, with jet black hair and beautiful dark eyes, slim of figure and quick to smile. She was accompanied by her nineteen-year-old brother, Aram, who kept a watchful eye and introduced her to his friends in the club.

Nadia asked a family friend about the "Jewish fellow" who was staring at her from across the room.

"Oh, he's not Jewish, he is Armenian," the friend explained. "He kind of looks Jewish because of that big nose. I think some hoodlums broke his nose in a fight years ago when he was hanging around in one of the casinos."

"Probably there was a girl involved," Nadia commented.

George walked over and had a mutual friend make introductions; then he asked the brother if he could escort Nadia and show her around the club. That was how they met. George was involved with the theater group that produced ethnic plays for the Armenians who frequented the international district. Occasionally George would direct and even perform. He kept trying to persuade Nadia to become an actor in the group. But she was too shy and self conscious. Besides, his real motive for recruiting her into the group was to see her more often.

A courtship followed that led to an engagement. Nadia delighted in telling her daughter years later that during that time, because she was unsure of her feelings for George in the beginning of their courtship, George had to work extra hard to convince her to give him a chance. He would write her "love

Nadia

letters," and she would tear them up and "sprinkle the pieces on him from the top of the stairs in her home when he came to call. But he was persistent and finally won her heart.

The engagement went on for seventeen months. During those months, George became well acquainted with the Oganjanovs and was particularly interested in the stories of the father, Haig.

In his youth Haig had been a soldier and prospector. He had studied to be an engineer but eventually joined the family business and became a successful business man. But now the family had fallen on hard times; the Japanese occupation in Harbin was interfering with their business. Haig moved the family to Shanghai because it was still a free port and the Japanese were more liberal. Everyone knew about World War II in Europe, but no one believed that the Japanese would attack America.

Nadia enjoyed telling stories about her family adventures. She told George how they had traveled from Kars, Armenia, to Irkutsk, Siberia. During the Russian Civil War in Siberia they had all escaped to Manzhouli, Manchuria, and then moved to Harbin in Northern China. Nadia and George knew many of the same people but didn't meet until that day at the Armenian Club.

It had taken Nadia's family more than twenty years to cross Asia. Now that they were in Shanghai, they were hoping to find a way to get to America. But World War II was on the horizon—yet another obstacle blocking their path.

As George sat in the social club and listened to the stories of his fiancée's family adventures, he realized that Haig the father and his family had followed the same path as so many Harbinites who had escaped Armenia to avoid the massacres and the ethnic wars—the same path George had followed before ending up in Shanghai. It was the story of a family struggling together in the midst of civil war, occupation, banditry and revolution. Like so many, they were searching for a place where they could finally be free from nationalistic fanatics, war, and subjugation.

At its most basic level, this was a story of a merchant who was never comfortable working for others. The struggle to save the family began with Haig's father Mkrtich in Kars, Armenia, when the first ethnic cleansing of the twentieth century forced the family into Asia. To tell their story, one had to go back to World War I and 1915 once more.

Part II

A FAMILY OF KARS
1918 to 1940

Part II

A FAMILY OF KARS

1918 to 1940

Chapter 14

Armenian Origins

To better understand the heritage, culture and customs of the Armenians, it is necessary to go back to the beginning and try to explain their origins.

Herodotus, the fifth century B.C. historian, wrote that the Armenians originally lived in Thrace in Greece. From Thrace they crossed into Phrygia in Asia Minor. They first settled in Phrygia, and then gradually migrated west of the Euphrates River to what became Armenia. Their language resembled that of the Phrygians, while their names, dress and customs was close to the Medes.

In other words, according to the ancient Greeks, the Armenians were not the original inhabitants of Asia Minor. They appear to have arrived sometime between the Phrygian migration to Asia Minor that followed the collapse of the Hittite Empire in the thirteenth century B.C. and the Cimmerian invasion of the Kingdom of Urartu in the eighth century B.C. Urartu is traditionally known as the landing site for the Ark of Noah after the great biblical flood of Genesis; the landing site was identified as Ararat in the Hebrew language and Urartu in Assyrian.

The present day capital of Armenia, Yerevan (or Erevan) is on an ancient site of a fortress-city (Erebuni) built by the Urartian king Argishti I in 782 B.C. The city was built as protection against the Cimmero-Scythian invasions that attempted to alter the power structure of the region. The eventual decline of Urartu enabled the proto-Armenians to establish themselves as the principal occupants of the region.

Modern archeology provides incomplete evidence of the possible origins of the Armenians. But most scholars believe that the Armenians were an Indo-European group who came into the area from one of two sources. Either they came with the proto-Iranians from the Aral Sea region, or they arrived from the Balkans with the Phrygians after the fall of the Hittites. They share some common elements of culture and language with the Hittites, who controlled lands across this region. For example, some scholars point to the word Hai (pronounced 'high'), the Armenian word for 'Armenian,' as derived from the Hai-yos (Hattian). In other words, the Armenians may have adopted the name of the Hittite empire as part of their assimilation during their migration over Hittite lands.

Other academics from Armenia argue in favor of a more nationalistic explanation: that the Armenians are the native inhabitants of historic Armenia. Archeologists have found evidence that since 1,000 B.C., this region has been the home of a distinct people dwelling in the high deserts near Ararat. Ararat—a 16,000-foot mountain easily seen from most of present day western Armenia—is the traditional site of the resting place of Noah's ark as described in Genesis 8:4, and for centuries archeologists have been searching for evidence of the ark in this area. Noah and his family were required by God to re-establish humanity from this region around Mount Ararat; therefore, many Armenians regard themselves as the "sons of Noah" or the ancestors of humanity.

Whatever the origin, the Armenians of 400 B.C. managed to consolidate their rule over Urartu and assimilate most of the original inhabitants to form the Armenian nation. The first acknowledged Armenian royal dynasty was the Orontids, ruling Armenia as a satrapy of the Persian Empire in the 4th century B.C.—around the time of Alexander the Great. Because geographically this region is a crossroads between warring empires, it has been the site of repeated conflict. In ancient times the region has been subjugated at one time or another by Babylonia, Persia, the Seleucid and the Romans.

But for the most part, 'subjugation' meant the paying of tribute in return for relative autonomy and protection. So long as the ancient rulers were willing to bow down to a superior empire and pay their taxes, they were allowed to rule their kingdom with little interference. The political intrigues of empires and how these empires sought to control various small kingdoms have always been an important part of the history of Armenia.

Chapter 15

In the Time of the Romans

Two hundred years after Alexander the Great had conquered Persia and the known world, a king of Persia named Mithradates II extended the Parthian empire to new territories. The empire included the Indus River in the east, which flows through Afghanistan and Iran to the Oxus River in the north and south to the Persian Gulf. In the west it extended to Anatolia (modern day Turkey).

At this time in the west Greece had been supplanted by Rome as the superpower of the region. And Mithradates II was the first Parthian king to come into contact with the Romans, exchanging ambassadors and establishing boundaries and alliances.

After Mithradates II, the kings were Sinaturkes (80-69 B.C.), Phrates III (69-57 B.C.) and Orodes II (57-37 B.C.). During the reign of Orodes II, the Roman proconsul of the east, Crassus set out to subjugate the Parthian empire. This was the same Crassus who had destroyed the slave revolt led by the slave Spartacus.

Crassus crossed the Euphrates River and entered Parthian territory to defeat the army of the Parthian Satrap (governor). The central Parthian army under General Suren attacked the Romans and in the battle of Carrhae (53 B.C.), the Roman army was crushed. The Parthians refrained from chasing the Romans beyond the Euphrates. Thus began a period of conflict with Rome that would last for years.

In 37 B.C., Mark Anthony, a general under Julius Caesar, attacked Parthia and like Crassus suffered a resounding defeat from the Parthian army. Again the Parthians remained east of the Euphrates River.

During the reign of Phrates IV (38-2 B.C.) while Augustus, the heir of

Julius Caesar, was consul of Rome, Rome and Parthia became friends again. Phrates V (2 B.C.-4 A.D.) was king of Parthia at the time of Jesus' birth in Palestine.

During the reign of Vologese I (51-80 A.D.), when Nero was emperor of Rome, another bitter war was waged over control of Armenia. After several Parthian victories, Rome agreed that Vologeses' brother Tiridates would be king of Armenia. Tiridates and Vologese were devout Zoroastrians and during this time Zoroastrianism became the official religion of Armenia. Vologese I even ordered the collection of all the oral and written texts of the Zoroastrian religion, which had been scattered since the time of Alexander's invasion.

With Tiridates as king, Armenia was now seen as a buffer state between the powerful empires of Rome and Parthia (Persia). To control the situation, both empires moved between diplomacy and border wars. For long periods, neither empire required more from the Armenian king than subjugation, which was limited to tribute, allowing the region to remain relatively autonomous.

Chapter 16

The First Christian State

Armenia's culture and national identity are closely entwined with its religiosity. It is a source of pride to Armenians to declare themselves the first Christian state during the golden age of Rome, even before Roman Catholicism. For most of its history, Armenia was under the control of kings of Parthia (Persia), emperors of Rome, sultans, and various other conquerors. And despite possible origins in Thrace or the Balkans, over time the Armenians were less Hellenistic and more closely allied to the Persians by habit, custom, culture and early religion. They readily accepted a Persian identity. However, the Persians were Zoroastrians and like the Romans, worshipped multiple gods and goddesses. The story of how Armenia embraced Christianity and became a semi-autonomous Christian state despite its many conquering neighbors must be considered when explaining the development of the Armenian character.

The story of the birth of Christianity is well known. The immaculate birth of Jesus in Bethlehem, a son of a carpenter from Nazareth who grows up to be a young teacher preaching a new message of salvation, hope and love unlike any other heard in Judea. The miracles that the teacher performed, the parables that made complex questions easier to understand, the envy of the authorities, the conspiracy to get rid of the popular teacher even as he gathered more followers, and then the horrid execution by the Romans and the miraculous resurrection.

After the resurrection, Jesus revealed himself to his disciples and followers. Many began to worship him as a manifestation of God on Earth, and Christianity was born.

But the biblical tale of Christianity blossoming from the death and resurrection of Christ to become a dominant world religion usually misses an important timeline. What many people do not realize is that for nearly three hundred years after Christ, Christianity was regarded by the known world as a cult, a bizarre aberration of Judaism.

There were rumors that Christians drank blood (the blood of Christ represented by wine), and ate flesh (the body of Christ represented by unleavened bread). That they sacrificed the innocent and held bizarre festivals. Persecution of Christians was common. Christianity was resisted by the establishment as the Christians tried to replace established festivals and holidays with their own. This new religion threatened the status quo.

Then, in 252 A.D., the assassination of a king in Armenia led to the exile of a Parthian prince who was destined to become a Christian and bring a new religion to Armenia. It was this isolated event that transformed Christianity from a cult to an established religion that gained acceptance across the known world.

Khosrov II of Armenia was assassinated by a Parthian agent named Anak under orders from Persia. The Parthians were jealous of the close ties Armenia had with Rome and hoped that the resulting chaos of the assassination would provide an opportunity to take control of the Armenian kingdom. The king's son and successor Tiridates III was an infant, but the many princes of the country formed a coalition that was able to hold the country together and—with the help of Rome—successfully resist the Persians. After several years, Anak was captured and executed along with most of his family, but two of his infant sons were rescued to Caesarea in Cappadocia (modern Kayseri, Turkey). One of those sons of Anak was the infant Gregory, born about 257 A.D.

Tiridates and Gregory

The Armenian princes who acted collectively as regent for the infant king sent Tiridates III to be raised and educated in Rome. There the young Tiridates won the friendship of the Roman emperor Diocletian by foiling a palace plot. The emperor agreed to appoint him king of Armenia, and a Roman-Armenian alliance began. Tiridates III, son of the slain king, raised an army and with the help of the Roman emperor finally drove the Persians out of Armenia in 287 A.D. The emperor Diocletian left the Armenian state as an independent protectorate under the rule of Tiridates. But the emperor, who was concerned about the early Christian influence on his subjects, convinced Tiridates to persecute and bear hostility toward all Christian followers.

By this time there had been Christian communities in Armenia for decades, established by the preaching of two apostles, St. Thaddeus and St.

Bartholomew. But because of oppression by the Romans and the Armenian royalty, the early Christians prayed and worshipped in secret. The Persian religion Zoroastrianism was the established norm.

Meanwhile, Gregory was educated in the Greek culture and became a Christian in his youth. He married into a noble family in Caesarea and had two sons. Then in about 280 A.D. he returned to Armenia and vowed to atone for his father's sin and fulfill his vision of establishing Christianity as a state religion. He joined the Armenian army and worked as a secretary to the new king. The traditional story is that the two men became good friends, and Tiridates did not immediately know that it was Gregory's father who had killed Tiridates' father.

By the time Gregory proclaimed his Christian faith and declared a holy mission, there was already a strong Christian presence in the country. The king's advisors, worried about the influence the young holy man might have on their king, sent out spies to investigate and soon discovered that he was the son of Anak. Lest they be accused of jealousy, the advisors did not expose Gregory immediately, but waited for the right time to reveal the evidence. That time came during a religious festival.

Tiridates, who followed Zoroastrianism and worshiped various ancient gods, insisted that Gregory place a flower wreath at the foot of a statue of the goddess Anahit during a pagan religious ceremony. Gregory refused and declared that his Christian faith would not allow him to worship false idols. The king was infuriated by what he perceived as sacrilege. It was then that several of the king's advisors informed him that Gregory was in fact the son of Anak, the traitor who had killed the king's father. Gregory was arrested for heresy and treason.

Gregory was tortured and finally thrown into a deep underground dungeon, Khor Virap (literally deep pit). A great boulder was rolled over the only entrance and the holy man was sealed alive in the tomb. As further punishment, King Tiridates then began a systematic subjugation of Christians and their cultish religion.

During the years following Gregory's imprisonment, persecution of Christians ebbed and flowed with the mood of the authorities. It was now three hundred years after the birth of Christ and Christianity was still viewed with suspicion. At this time, a group of virgin nuns came to Armenia fleeing the Roman persecution of their Christian faith. The leader of the nun's order, Gayane, had heard that the Armenians were, if not supportive, at least tolerant of Christians. However, among the nuns in the order was a great beauty named Ripsime. Told of the nuns and the beauty of Ripsime, Tiridates brought them all to his palace. Seeing the beautiful virgin, he tried to force her to become one of his wives, but Ripsime refused his advances. So the king tortured and killed all of them.

Soon after, the king fell ill with a mysterious ailment that caused him to behave like a wild animal. He would growl and foam at the mouth, run aimlessly through the forest, tear at his own skin and cover himself in filth. He would tear off his clothes and attack even those he knew. Modern medicine would undoubtedly identify this ailment as lycanthropy (the origin of the werewolf stories). Legend says that the illness was God's wrath for the sins committed against the early Christians. The palace royalty was understandably concerned that the kingdom would be lost if the Romans or the Persians discovered that the king had gone mad and turned into a beast. In fact, the Roman emperor had already signed a secret treaty with the Sassanids of Persia to invade Armenia.

During these desperate times, the king's sister Khosrovidoukht had a dream. She insisted that the dream was a vision and must be obeyed. But the dream was preposterous. In her dream, Gregory, the king's friend from long ago, would emerge from his dungeon and cure the king of this malady.

Now Gregory had been put in Khor Virap twelve years earlier. No one had seen him after the great stone had been rolled over the pit. The king's advisers were all certain that he was long dead. But the sister insisted that they find him, and riders were sent to the pit to investigate. The boulder that had sealed the section of the underground dungeon where Gregory was imprisoned was removed. To everyone's amazement, Gregory emerged from Khor Virap, pale and drawn but with his spirit and faith unbroken.

Apparently a relative in a nearby village had been bringing a loaf of bread every day for all those years and delivering it through a hole at the top of Khor Virap. This was how Gregory had sustained himself. Although severely emaciated, he had not lost his courage or his faith. When he was told of the king's malady, he immediately asked to see him.

After Gregory was brought before the king, he prayed and asked God to forgive Tiridates for the many sins he had committed. The king was miraculously cured of his illness. Moreover, when he regained his senses, the king realized that it was the Christian faith that had saved him. This miracle and the treachery of his former friend, the Roman emperor Diocletian, convinced Tiridates to support Gregory's holy mission to convert the country.

In 301 A.D., Tiridates and many in his royal court were officially baptized by Gregory. The king proclaimed Christianity as the official state religion of Armenia. And so, Tiridates III was the first monarch to officially adopt Christianity. His example and Gregory's work evangelizing the countryside would inspire other nations seeking conversion to Christianity.

The king soon appointed Gregory as Catholicos of the Armenian Apostolic Church and Gregory was consecrated by neighboring bishops in Cappadocia as patriarchal bishop of Armenia, first bishop of Armenia. All this took place about twenty years before the rest of the known world began to accept Christianity as an established religion.

During these twenty years Armenia became a sanctuary for all persecuted Christians from across the Roman Empire, until the resignation of Diocletian and the ascendency of Constantine. Constantine I spent most of his reign consolidating the Roman Empire under his rule. But his acceptance of Christian beliefs eased the persecution that had been so prevalent during Diocletian's time.

Gregory subsequently evangelized parts of the country remaining under Roman control and influenced Christianity in Albania, Georgia and other regions of the Caucasus Mountains. He established new churches in Western Armenia and began the construction of the Cathedral of the Mother Church in the capital city of Echmiadzin.

After Gregory died in about 332 A.D., he was canonized as a saint and proclaimed as Gregory the Illuminator. His corpse was dismembered and distributed as holy relics. His head is believed to be in Italy, while his mummified left hand is still at Echmiadzin in Armenia—where it is used in ceremonies to consecrate new bishops.

The Emperor Constantine legalized Christianity with the Edict of Milan and later called the Council of Nicea to resolve the schisms that had formed within the various factions of Christian communities, thus unifying the religion. It was Gregory's son who represented the Armenian Apostolic Christian state at the Council of Nicea. In 337 A.D. Constantine was baptized on his deathbed and declared that Rome should become a Christian state.

It was the establishment of Armenia as a Christian state that made the people and culture distinct and unique. And while some nations have survived by accepting and adopting the religious ideas of conquerors and invaders as part of their assimilation, the Armenians have retained their distinct national identity primarily because of their ties to Christianity.

Ironically, the beginning of the disintegration of the Armenian Kingdom is sometimes marked from the time shortly after the country became Christian. After Tiridates, many of the aristocratic families, each adopting their own interpretation of the religion, abandoned the defense of the kingdom and retreated into the mountainous valleys. Without unified leadership, the kingdom was soon divided between the Persians and the Romans.

The new religion introduced an element of dissension and political discord. The Apostolic Church was vehemently opposed to the Greek Orthodoxy of the Byzantines and fostered enemies among the pagans of Persia and much later the Arab Muslims.

Moreover, as schisms formed within the Christian religion and the Apostolic Church broke with the Roman Church, Armenia split into

Orthodox, Protestant and Catholic sects. These sects formed rival religious and political organizations that created alliances with factions that would lead to conflict. It was these factional alliances as much as anything that helped to bring great misfortune to the people and the State.

Because geographically Armenia stood as a passage from Europe to the Middle East, it became the target of conquerors who encountered little organized resistance. The country was the scene of constant strife. And yet, the breakup of the kingdom into independent enclaves each ruled by a local prince provided a sense of independence and self reliance that preserved the Armenian identity for centuries after the kingdom was gone.

Chapter 17

Armenian Nobility

The nobility issue has always played an important role in Armenian society. It goes back to ancient times, when nobility was a reward for service to the king or provincial prince or a result of alliance by marriage. Many Armenian noble houses were linked to the proto-Iranian nobility through dynastic marriages.

A small minority of nobles were created to facilitate assimilation with foreign families predominantly of titled Indo-European origin from Persians, Medes, Greeks and Romans. But the majority of the nobility had Armenian origins—men granted noble titles by special decree of medieval kings for their services to the royal court.

Within the Armenian nobility was an internal hierarchy. The apex or head was the king, which in Armenian is arqa. The term arqa originates from the common Aryan root for monarch.

The sons of the king or the princes were called sepuh. The eldest son or heir and crown prince was called avag sepuh. In the case of royal death, the crown prince would automatically inherit the crown. Occasionally, when no crown prince was designated, a grand duke was appointed to serve as regent or titular head of state.

There was a second layer of bdeshkhs or provincial rulers. The third layer—after the king and his family and the bdeshkhs—was composed of lesser princes called ishkhans. They would have hereditary estates and head princely houses.

Finally, in the modern age, a variety of new noble titles existed within different provinces. In the Artsakh province the equivalent for ishkhan (prince) was melik. These were the aristocrats of the new age. Those meliks who were politically influential represented the derebeys that governed a region for the Ottomans or the Persian Sultan (depending on who controlled a specific region at a specific time in history). The derebeys or valley lords became virtually independent of the Ottoman central government; the local governing was left to the meliks.

Slowly a caste culture began to evolve that consisted of farmers, laborers, merchants and a noble class with various gradations.

The aristocratic tradition in Armenia suffered during the post Russian Revolution because of the annexation of eastern Armenia by the Bolshevik regime of Russia. The nobility was dissolved as a social class and the Armenian aristocracy suffered systematic oppression.

Some families preserved their traditions and history by leaving the Communist regime and moving to other countries. Others simply hid their royal titles.

Chapter 18

Haig and Arpenik

Haig could trace his ancestry to the 1600s, because most of his people were from Kars or had stayed within a short distance of this town in Western Armenia. Haig was born in 1893 in Kars, Armenia, and died in 1977. During the course of his life he witnessed genocide, fought in World War I, and survived several Asian revolutions. During his travels, he experienced the Communist Civil War and foreign occupation by the Japanese, and was in Shanghai during the Second World War.

As a young man, he studied to be an engineer. There are photographs of him proudly wearing his school uniform decorated with the engineering epaulets of the academy where he studied. During his life he enjoyed designing and building tools and furniture and inventing useful gadgets.

He was a stout, broad-shouldered man with dark eyes and a heavy mustache common to the period. Later in life he would shave his head, which would accent a broad round face with ferocious eyes and heavy eyebrows.

Haig had five sisters. One in particular shared several adventures in Northern China. Her name was Haiganoush, and she had two children, Talia and Arshalois.

The other sisters were: Siranoush, Shohokat, Arovsiak, and Betheme, all born in Kars.

Haig's wife was Arpenik Melik-Stepanian, born in 1897 in Djulfa. She was a member of an aristocratic family, while Haig was the son of a wealthy merchant. She was short and delicate but in no way shy. She seemed very direct and at ease in any situation. Later in life, with hair pulled back tight on her head, she had the look of a stern schoolmarm. And yet almost everyone who knew her saw her as bright and effervescent. She had a ready laugh and

Haig in Engineering School Uniform

rarely had a bad word to say about anyone. Haig fell in love with her as soon as they met.

Haig's father owned a large mill and supplied flour to the entire town of Kars, plus the surrounding villages. It was during the course of business that Haig met the Stepanians and was immediately attracted to their daughter, Arpenik. They fell in love and decided to marry. Originally, Arpenik's father Stepanian opposed her marrying Haig. He looked down on the Oganjanovs as merchants or business people from Kars, which they were. But she (Arpenik) was a melik. This was a higher class title, an aristocratic title. According to the caste system of the day, marriage to a merchant was beneath her social standing. They married despite the family objections.

Haig's Children

After Haig and Arpenik were married, they had two daughters in Kars.

Their first child was Isabella, born in Kars, Armenia in 1916. She graduated as a professional dentist in China. As a young woman, she traveled throughout central China on a hospital train to bring modern dentistry to the rural countryside.

Haig and Arpenik in 1921

When she immigrated to America, her dentistry credentials were not recognized. After a thirty year interruption, she returned to school to become certified to practice dentistry in the United States. Late in her life, she organized and ran a free clinic in Chicago until she retired.

She married Suren Pashinian, a businessman she met in the Orient, and had two sons, Aroutium and Ambartsoum, both born in the Orient in 1940.

The second child Nadejda (Russian for 'hope') was born in Kars, Armenia, in 1918. Nadia married George in 1942 in Shanghai. They had one son and one daughter, both born in Shanghai during the war.

Later, after Haig and his family traveled across Asia, they settled in Irkutsk,

Isabelle

Siberia, for ten years. Haig and Arpenik had three more children—Aram, Grikor and Nicolas—born in the city of Irkutsk.

Aram, born in 1921, became a merchant seaman and traveled the world before settling down in Canada. He married Valerie Hughes in Canada in 1951.

After Aram left the merchant marines, he graduated from college with advanced degrees in Oriental languages and became a professor of Slavic studies at the University of British Colombia. They had one daughter, Arpenik (Penny), who was born in 1953 in Vancouver, Canada.

The second son, Grikor, died as a child in Irkutsk.

Nick Haig was the youngest child. He was born in 1926. After extensive travel through Asia, particularly in New Zealand, he immigrated to America. His wife was Josephine Alexanoff. He became a successful businessman in America under the name Nick Ohan. They had three daughters—Sandy, Isabel and Virginia—and one son, Nick, Jr.

This is the lineage of the family that defines Nadia's ancestry. The stories recounted here are centered on Mkrtich Ohanjanian and his son, Haig. But some of the stories going back several hundred years told by Haig about his ancestors are part of the family's oral history and folklore.

The first ancestor remembered by the family was Ohan.

Ohan Meitarjian was born in 1770 in Kars, Armenia, and died in 1860. His wife, Miriam, was born in 1772. He was nicknamed Ohanjan because of his kind nature and likable personality. There are numerous family stories told about him. Ohanjan had three children—Grikor, Arakel and Javair. Following the custom of the day, the sons took the father's first name and added "ian."

The oldest was Grikor Ohanjanian, born in 1795. He was a farmer in Kars and a volunteer in the Russo-Turkish War of 1826. Grikor's wife was Oskihat, who was born in 1805. Grikor died in 1897.

Grikor and Oskihat had three children—Nazar, Ohannes and Mkrtich. So, a direct descendant of Ohanjan was Mkrtich Oganjanov (Russian version of Ohanjanian), who was born in Kars around 1873 and died in Irkutsk in 1923. Mkrtich's wife was Gayane Eckmalian. They had six children who survived to adulthood: five daughters and one son—Haig. Haig was Nadia's father.

Aram (far right) and Nick (left) behind Haig.

Chapter 19

Kars, Armenia

The town of Kars is situated at an altitude of 1750 meters on the foothills that lead to greater Mt. Ararat located southeast of Kars. Mount Ararat is actually composed of two peaks (greater and lesser Ararat) with the highest standing at 5,165 meters (16,000 feet). The mountains in this region are volcanic, though no eruptions have been recorded in human history.

The area surrounding Kars is dry, barren and lightly inhabited. The word 'Kars' is a contraction of 'snowy water' in the Turkish dialect because the winters are long and very cold. Deforestation, drought, overgrazing and destructive earthquakes have impacted the region severely, and it is now sparsely populated. Yet this region is one of the oldest human settlements in Anatolia and an archeologist's garden—with numerous pre-historic remains.

Dating back centuries, the archeological site called Ani is located forty-two kilometers east of Kars, near the present border between Armenia and Turkey. While a historical ruin now, Ani was once a center of commerce with a population of over 100,000. Ani and Kars were intermittent capitals of the Bagatrid Kingdom, a dominant Armenian state during the Ninth and Tenth Centuries, and they both suffered numerous invasions. They were invaded in the early eleventh century by Turks and then later by the Mongols. Ani was nearly destroyed by earthquake in the fourteenth century and sacked by Tamerlane in 1386. Later, in the sixteenth century, it was rebuilt by the Ottoman Turks. It was reduced to ruin by the Persians in 1604 and rebuilt again.

Finally Ani declined into ruin. Trade routes began to move farther south and Kars became the capital of the province of the same name. Today the site of Ani is surrounded by crumbling ramparts and towers. Inside the walls are the remains of several Armenian churches with amazing frescos, a Cathedral, a Georgian church, a monastery, a ruined Seljuk palace and a couple of mosques. Under Turkish military control, it is advertised as a tourist attraction. Visitors can obtain permits in Kars to see the ruins.

Kars has been distinctive for its isolation and independence from the major powers of the region. It was the city-province farthest from Constantinople, the capital of the Ottomans, and farthest from Tehran, the capital of the Persians, and farthest from Moscow, the capital of Russia. During the nineteenth century this region was the center of many Russian-Persian-Turkish conflicts and changed hands repeatedly. In fact, one of Haig's ancestors was known to have witnessed the occupation of Kars by both Persians and Turks. Several of his ancestors were volunteers in these border conflicts.

Then in 1878 the territory was ceded to Russia and Kars became a city state of Tsarist Russia. It was during this era when the Ohanjanian family lived there. Until after World War I, Kars was considered part of the Republic of Armenia as a protectorate of Russia. But after the Russian Revolution, a peace treaty was signed between the nationalist government of Kemal Ataturk and the USSR. The city of Kars was given to Turkey as one of the treaty conditions. The transfer to Turkish rule probably influenced the immigration of Haig's family to Siberia. By this time they may have considered themselves more aligned with Russia than Turkey or Western Armenia. And ethnic nationalism was creating violence and chaos in the region.

Life during the Collapse of the Ottoman Empire

The conditions of life for the Armenians living in the Ottoman Empire became of international interest after 1878. Before that and long before the deportation of Armenians in the twentieth century, the Armenian population in the Empire was made up of four distinct castes.

There was the wealthy aristocracy known as the amiras, who were well removed from the general population of the region.

Then there were the traders, merchants and artisans in the towns of the Empire, who were well integrated with the Muslim populations in the large towns.

In the outlying areas of the countryside, there were the villagers—for centuries they were the farming peasantry who lived off the soil and from the flocks they tended. They were typically deep in debt to the local Turkish or Kurdish derebeys. Because they lived in isolated villages and constituted the bulk of the population in a region, the peasantry was rarely exposed to any other Muslim influence other than usury. In fact, except for taxation, there were many wholly Armenian villages on the plains of Erzerum and Moush that did not intermingle for years.

And finally, there were the mountaineers. These were a people who had led a bold, semi-independent existence untouched by the empire and its tax collectors. These included the regions of Zeitun and Cilicia and the inhabitants of the Sasun—a confederation of forty Armenian villages.

The mountaineers were a tough and hardy breed, masters of their own affairs. Even though they would pay tribute to the local Kurdish derebeys, they were virtually untouched by the central government of the Empire.

It was this lack of contact among the peasantry and the isolation of the mountaineers that encouraged these regions to regard themselves as an independent Armenia state. The lack of contact also began to foster a nationalistic spirit among the Armenians. As the Ottoman Empire declined, the rulers began to view the Armenians with suspicion.

And yet within the townships in the modern age, it was a different story. In the nineteenth century, the several populated regions in Armenia and particularly in Turkish Armenia had become heavily intermingled with the Kurds and Turks. In some of these regions, the Armenians may have been outnumbered by the combined populations of Kurds and Turks, but these two peoples had significantly different outlooks and aspirations and should not be counted together. Many scholars believe that in other places, such as the province of Van, the Armenians constituted a majority of the combined total of the peoples.

Overall the Armenians were a large proportion of the general population of the region even when in the minority.

In the late 1800s the estimated population of Armenians throughout the Ottoman Empire was 2.4 million, and they constituted a majority in Kurdistan and the Erzerum province, which included Kars. By 1912—when Haig was living in Kars—it is estimated that the Turks were twenty-five percent of the population, the Kurds, sixteen percent, and the Armenians, thirty-nine percent. The rest were Assyrians, Greeks, Azeri, and Yezidis.

Relations between the Armenians and their Turkish and Kurdish Muslim neighbors differed in each locality. All the towns and many of the villages were mixed Muslim/Christian. Typically there was a Muslim ruling class reporting to a valley lord or central authority, and an Armenian merchant and entrepreneurial class under the control of either a melik or a church patriarch. Many Armenians even served in public office. In addition, there were many Muslims who were mostly pastoral and isolated, living on the slopes of the hills above the plains, occupying themselves with their flocks.

So Muslims were at the top and the bottom of the social scale, with the Armenian Christians occupying the middle. When nationalistic sentiment erupted and rumors started to circulate of alliances with the British and Russians, the central government responded to the threat with violence. They began a campaign to disarm and destroy the minority Armenian population.

Chapter 20

The Conscription of Garabed

During times of war or civil strife, the illegal deeds done by the State for the sake of national pride or security are terrible and beyond imagining. Such troubled times can result in the ultimate horror in human interactions. Between 1914 and 1922 the crumbling Ottoman Empire and the new nationalist Turkish government began a program to actively destroy the Armenian population under Turkish control. Large numbers of the population were gathered together and their property confiscated. Many were driven on foot into the Der Dzor desert. Bands of Turks and Kurds were encouraged to attack the unarmed victims. The murderous deportation lasted through the duration of World War I. By 1922, it has been estimated that 1.5 million Armenians were killed, kidnapped or displaced. The real number of victims may never be known. But the deportation was effective and used later as a blueprint by subsequent governments in the twentieth century to control or destroy their minority population by mass deportation.

It was the ambition of various Armenian political parties in the minority settlements to establish an independent state. The Tsarist Russian authorities in St. Petersburg—who were encouraging insurrection within the Ottoman Empire and seeking access to the Caspian, Black and Mediterranean Seas—promoted the idea of an independent state. Several political parties of the Armenian minority began to attain significance. By 1887, Armenians in Geneva had founded the first Armenian party that emphasized Marxist principles. The Hunchaks drew their membership almost entirely from Russian Armenians. The Federation of Armenian Revolutionaries or Dashnaks appeared later as an umbrella organization for various nationalistic groups. The political groups that emerged in the twentieth century, particularly the

Hunchaks and the Dashnaks, were competing for the favor of the Armenians, with the Hunchaks stressing their socialist convictions while the Dashnaks put more emphasis on nationalistic views.

In the First World War, the Ottoman Empire fought on the side of the Central Powers—Germany, Austria, Hungary, and Bulgaria—against the Entente powers—England, France and their allies. Later the conflict extended to the Russians and the Arabs. Later still, America joined Britain and France. The year 1914 was pivotal. In early 1914, before the Ottomans had entered the war, there was already suspicion that political groups were collaborating with enemies of the Ottoman Empire. By the fall of 1914, the Russians were promising to free the Armenians from the tyranny that had ruled over them for 500 years.

Then, when war broke out in Europe, the Ottoman authorities were grappling with the problem that Constantinople was threatened by the French and British fleets in the Dardanelles on the one hand and by the Russians on the Eastern front on the other.

The Ottomans decided to take action to settle old scores and save their crumbling Empire from any possible insurrection by the Armenians by deporting all minority Armenians living in Turkey.

Armenians the world over remember April 24, 1915, as the day the genocide of the Armenians began. The Ottoman Minister of the Interior, Talaat Pasha, sent a telegram on 24 April 1915, ordering the arrest of insurrectionists. The coded telegram first went to the governors of the provinces affected by Armenian insurrection and ordered that all political organizations be closed, all documents found should be confiscated, and all leaders and prominent members should be arrested.

In the telegram, Talaat Pasha, stated the following:

> These rebellions and the decision of the Dashnak Committee, after the outbreak of war, immediately to incite the Armenians in Russia against us, and to have the Armenians in the Ottoman state rebel with all their force when the Ottoman army is at its weakest, are all acts of treason, which would affect the life and future of the country …. You are therefore ordered to close down immediately all branches within your province of the Hunchak, Dashnak, and similar committees … All weapons should be confiscated, and all files and documents in the course of proper execution of these orders are to be turned over to the military courts.

The orders included that Armenians, whose presence in one area was considered to be inappropriate, should be transferred to other parts of the province, so as not to give them the opportunity to engage in harmful acts. In the end, these operations were extended to include not only those who might resist, but everyone—all men, women and children as well.

The Turkish justification has always been to point to the many subsequent examples of deportation as a wartime necessity. They remind their critics of the deportation of Muslims by the Russians, the deportation of Jews by various governments, the deportation of Native Americans and Japanese Americans by the U.S. government, the deportation of Germans by the French and the general movement of any minority that might constitute a danger to the majority. The Turkish government stated, "It is undoubtedly true that many innocent people lost their property, their health, and even their lives in the relocation of 1915—many Armenians. But trying to place blame for a wartime tragedy such as this is senseless."

However, it is clear that the reaction of the Ottoman government to the possibility of insurrection by the minority population was completely out of proportion. The government action resulted in the annihilation of whole sections of the Armenians within Turkey. In early 1915 the Turks arrested a total of 235 suspected Armenian ringleaders, but subsequently slaughtered tens of thousands of unarmed civilians and over the next few years confiscated all property belonging to the Armenian minority. The goal of the government in inciting these deportations was clearly annihilation. The deportation, forced conversions, mass exiles and massacres that took place during the summer and autumn of 1915 completely depopulated many Armenian provinces within Turkey.

Not long after the Ottoman government began a systematic purging of the Armenian population in Turkey and Western Armenia, stories began to spread of atrocities committed against entire communities of unarmed civilians. Families who were slaughtered or split up sometimes had one survivor to testify to the tragedy.

One story told of Suren, who lost his entire family while away on business but years later found a sister, presumed dead, residing in an insane asylum, comatose. Another told of Assoghig, who lost his family as a child and was raised in a monastery to become a priest. Then there was Paul, who was five when he was found wandering in the desert after a long forced march where he witnessed his family die of starvation. After Paul was found, he was raised by a benefactor and brought to America. As the survivors told their stories, it became clear that these were not isolated instances of war but that this was ethnic mass murder. The conscription of Garabed was one of the tales told in detail by the witnesses of that time.

Garabed was born in Diyarbarkir near Maden (Mardin) in the southeastern part of Turkey in 1896. His father was a wealthy mine owner, well known in the region and respected. The region was rich with silver and copper and the father of the family leased the mines and hired workers to mine for copper. By any measure, Garabed was a child of privilege and wealth.

In 1914, Garabed was seventeen and planning to study medicine in Constantinople (later renamed Istanbul). He was making plans to go to school when the Ottoman government ordered a conscription of all young Armenians into the army to fight against the British, French and Russians. In spring of 1914, World War I had not yet begun, but the Czarist Russians were expanding their territorial claims in the north, while the British and their Arab allies were threatening Palestine and Damascus. The Turkish army claimed that it needed soldiers to fortify its military ranks.

Consequently, Garabed postponed his study of medicine in Constantinople to go to basic army training near his home town. There were already rumors of murder in some of the towns and cities where pockets of Armenians were suspected of collaborating with the British or the Russians and stories told of neighborhoods destroyed by the gendarmerie. But the troubles had not yet spread to Diyarbarkir, and Garabed was actually excited to become a soldier for the Empire. His only sense of foreboding came when he realized that everyone in his company was a minority—either Christian Turk or Armenian.

During basic training, he and his fellow conscripts were given uniforms and guns. The conscripts consisted of 120 men from the region. Then one night they were separated from the Turkish national soldiers ordered to surrender their rifles, marched into an isolated section of the nearby forest and ordered to dig a series of long trenches. They were told it was all part of the basic training.

The Ottoman government had issued orders to the provinces to isolate and deal with the minorities. The government considered the Turkish-Armenians to be as much of a threat to internal security as the invading forces from the north. So, after the trenches were dug, the arms of the conscripts were bound with ropes, and they were tied together, two by two.

Garabed was tied to an older fellow who immediately realized what was happening. He told the young man to jump into the pit as soon as the shooting started. Garabed and his friend did not wait; instead, during the confusion of screams and gunfire, they simultaneously jumped into the ditch, their arms still bound. The other conscripts were shot one by one and then dumped into the ditches. In the pit, Garabed and his friend lay still as the corpses piled on top of them. They had little air to breath in the ditch but they had avoided the bullets. However, the soldiers were not done. They stood over the ditch and used bayonets to stab the bodies to ensure that no one was left alive. They systematically stabbed each body and looked for signs of life.

By the time the soldiers were satisfied that the slaughter was complete it was dark, so they quickly threw dirt over the pits and departed with plans to return in the daylight to finish covering the trenches.

After the soldiers had left and it grew quiet, the long silence was broken by the voice of the conscript who had jumped into the ditch with Garabed. "Friend, are you still alive?" he asked. Garabed responded that indeed by some miracle he was. They had timed their leap into the pit to avoid being shot and were now covered by the dead. Both men managed to free their arms from the ropes and claw their way up out of the ditch by squeezing themselves through the entangled bodies of their comrades.

Garabed was covered in blood and wounded in the leg and the right side, but his friend was even more seriously hurt, for a bayonet thrust had punctured his chest and lung.

They ran to a nearby field, hoping to hide from the soldiers who were sure to return. They had walked a short distance when the other man collapsed. Garabed then realized how seriously his friend was wounded. He carried him deeper into the field and tore strips from his shirt to dress their wounds. But his friend's wounds were very deep and oozing blood. He had already bled a great deal and they both realized that Garabed's efforts were in vain. The comrade urged Garabed to leave him and save himself. "Do not worry about one more dead," he said, "but report this atrocity to anyone who will listen."

After hesitating for a time, Garabed accepted that his friend could not be rescued. Garabed kissed him softly on the forehead and bid him farewell. Although badly wounded himself and not retaining much hope of his own escape, he left his friend in the field and continued to limp away from the carnage of the previous night. Garabed crossed the field and decided to seek refuge in a depression thick with tall grass and weeds. He knew he could not travel by day and could not go back to his home. After remaining in hiding all day, he waited until it was very dark and began a journey to Maden, a major town eighty kilometers southeast of Diyarbarkir.

Maden was achingly far to travel by foot even for a man in good health, but for Garabed in his weakened state, the path to his destination felt endless. Walking mostly by night, he arrived near Maden and luckily ran into a Kurdish woman who took pity on him. She knew Garabed's father who was well respected in the area and for his sake, she offered him refuge in an animal shed on her small farm. Garabed remained hidden in the shed during the day and at night, the kind woman brought him food. Slowly his wounds began to heal.

Three weeks later, the woman told him that she could no longer hide him. The Russian Tsarist Army was advancing and the Turks were on patrol and suspicious of anyone who might be Armenian. The family was afraid for their own lives, since anyone harboring an Armenian would be killed on the spot.

The kind and generous woman handed Garabed a Kurdish outfit with a turban as a disguise. After giving him food and water, she bid him farewell and good luck. He walked during the dark and dangerous nights and hid wherever he could during the day. After the food was gone, he dared not beg for food from strangers for fear of being turned in. He was forced to eat anything he could find—grass roots, weed, bark—edible or not. After walking for several weeks, he finally reached the Russian Armenian battle lines.

Upon finally reaching the Russian border in his Kurdish outfit with no identification documents, Garabed was immediately arrested. He could not speak Russian and the soldiers decided that they had captured a spy or Kurdish smuggler. They tried to interrogate him, but all he could do was try to make them understand in Turkish or Armenian. Finally he began to physically make the sign of the cross across his chest. He had to do it several times before the Russians finally realized he was not a Muslim. They sent for an interpreter, who translated his explanation to the Russian authorities. Once they confirmed who he was, they allowed him to stay in occupied Armenia, and he eventually joined the Russian Army as an aide.

During the atrocities, most of Garabed's family was killed and their property confiscated. His parents, his older brother and his younger sister were murdered. An older sister Soghome, who was married but living with the family, never completely recovered from the horror of the death march in the desert of Der Dzor. She witnessed a soldier slash her pregnant younger sister with a saber, killing her and her unborn child. This was later reported by witnesses to be the most common method of execution against unarmed people by the Turkish soldiers. It saved bullets.

Meanwhile, as Garabed was recovering from his ordeal, Russia was being transformed by the Bolshevik Revolution. Garabed left Armenia and eventually found his way to Manchuria and then China with a flood of other Russian refugees.

By the time Garabed reached the town of Manzhouli on the Manchurian border, he was exhausted and ill again. Long periods of starvation during escape from Turkey had taken their toll. He landed in the hospital in Manzhouli and was soon tended by ladies from the Armenian Relief Society.

Whenever they gather, groups of Armenian ladies everywhere are notorious for matchmaking. Garabed was immediately recognized as a young, good-looking and available man in the community. Soon he was introduced to a lovely girl named Mariam who had recently arrived with her brothers. Mariam was in fact a cousin to the Oganjanov family. After a three month courtship, Mariam and Garabed married and shared many more adventures in the Orient.

Garabed suffered recurring illness for much of the rest of his life in Harbin. After a particularly long bout, he died at the age of forty-two in Harbin, Northern China. While trying to enter the United States after World War II, his wife and daughter traveled an extremely circuitous route and saw much of the world. In 1961 they finally succeeded in reaching America. The tale of Garabed's conscription was taken from the memoirs of Garabed's daughter Virginia Meltickian.

Chapter 21

The Family Leaves Kars (1918)

Haig, who was registered as Oganjanov (a Russian version of his Armenian name), had served in the Russian Tsarist Army during World War I. The family spoke Russian as a principal language and regarded themselves as Russian Armenians. During their travels through the newly formed Soviet Union of 1918, they used their Russianized name.

While most Armenians who fled their homeland left because of Turkish and Kurdish attacks in Turkey, others left for the eastern frontier during the Russian Civil War because of Bolshevik persecution. The Bolsheviks considered all property owners, merchants, business people, and royalty— regardless of personal fortune—as rich oppressors of the workers of the world.

They targeted anyone with money for collectivization and a redistribution of national wealth. They also went after the Bourgeois or middle class, whom they saw as the source of misery for the farming peasantry and laborers.

The Oganjanovs, whose main offenses were owning property and running successful businesses, became lumped in with the rich Bourgeois. When the Russian Revolution swept across Western Russia and Eastern Armenia, Mkrtich Oganjanov—Haig's father and patriarch of the family—decided to flee to the Orient.

His plan was to cross Asia from Kars to Manzhouli on the Manchurian-Siberia border. This was easier than trying to go west into Europe, which was torn by war and revolution and heavily guarded. The family would proceed to the seaport of Vladivostok on the Pacific coast or into Northern China and then down to Shanghai, a free port where visas were not required. From there they would buy passage to America.

The family embarked on a 4,000 mile journey from Kars, Armenia, to the town of Manzhouli (or Man-chu-li) in 1918.

Primarily they were running from Ottoman Turkish persecution in Kars. But the region was also engulfed in regional wars and the Communist revolution was throwing the whole of Asia into turmoil. The Communist influence had not quite reached Siberia and they got to Irkutsk hoping to wait until the chaos ended. Many in Eastern Europe and Russia found it easier to travel to the east and across the China border than to risk crossing west into war-torn Europe.

Because of the Russian Revolution, all transportation was unreliable, and the family traveled to their destination in a covered wagon. The wagon contained Mkrtich and Gayane—the patriarch and matriarch—their five daughters and one son, plus the son's family. The son Haig Nikitovich—in his late twenties and already a veteran of World War I—was traveling with his wife Arpenik Mihailovna and their two daughters, Isabella and Nadia, both infants. Two men, seven women, and two babies shared that wagon. They disguised themselves as gypsies and made the 4,000 mile journey by horse-drawn wagon.

Why gypsies? Because it was considered very bad luck to molest or offend gypsies.

The plan was to get to the eastern coast of Russia and find passage on a ship to America. Reports on the Civil War between the "Reds" and the "Whites" in Russia in 1918 indicated that the Communist takeover was faltering. A former admiral of the Tsarist Navy was in charge of the White Russian forces, and early on he had been successful in restricting the Bolsheviks in the West. He was concentrating his efforts on taking Siberia and splitting the country.

There were also rumors that European expeditionary forces and an American force were coming into Asia to protect the railroad and possibly segregate eastern Russia from European Russia. This gave the family hope that they might someday return home. But they needed someplace to wait out the revolution and the chaos of war. They decided to stop in Irkutsk rather than proceed straight onto the Pacific coast.

Chapter 22

Aleksander Kolchak

In 1918 a former admiral of the Tsarist Navy named Kolchak was in charge of the White Russian forces in Siberia. The career of Admiral Kolchak, particularly during his last few years in Siberia, provides a reasonable snapshot of the critical times after World War I in Russia.

Aleksander Kolchak was reportedly descended from a Bosnian Muslim and a wealthy family from southern Ukraine. Educated for a naval career, he distinguished himself both as an Arctic explorer and expert in defensive naval minefields. He honed his skills as a naval commander during the Russo-Japanese War of 1905 and by 1916 was promoted to vice admiral and fleet commander.

Tsarist Russia had joined Britain and France against Germany when the Bolshevik revolution broke out. The revolution was inspired by a mutiny against the Tsar. After the Bolsheviks seized power, they made plans to abandon the war against the Axis powers. Kolchak, who was abroad in the United States teaching underwater mine warfare tactics at the American Naval War College, was upset with the Bolsheviks for undermining naval authority and particularly unhappy about their avowed goal of dropping out of the war in Europe. He offered his services to the Americans but was routed by the British to Manchuria to protect the Chinese Eastern Railway.

As the Bolsheviks consolidated their control over Asia, Kolchak was asked to be the Supreme Ruler and head of the White Army. He had refused the post for a long time; he did not wish to accept such responsibility. Also, although he was a brilliant seaman, the Civil War in Russia was a land war.

Finally he promoted himself to Admiral and allied himself with the British. Initially Kolchak had numerous successes, including taking the city of Omsk in the steppes leading to Siberia. There was some hope that the Bolsheviks and Socialist-Revolutionary Directory (SR) would be pushed out of Eastern Russia.

But Kolchak aroused the dislike of key potential allies. He was irascible, not very patient with subordinates, and did not like to explain himself to his allied peers. His inability to control his temper was well known. He never abused his subordinates, but he often spoke in anger. His foreign allies included the Czech Legion, the Polish Division and the American Expeditionary Forces under commander William S. Graves, who was sent to protect the operation of the Trans-Siberian railroad. They all disliked his autocratic and royalist behavior, particularly Graves. Moreover, the Kolchak government had no one with experience or intelligence to run governmental affairs in Siberia.

When the Red forces managed to reorganize and turn the attack against Kolchak, his inexperience with land warfare and his political ineptitude with his allies were his undoing. He was handed over to the SR of Irkutsk by the Czecho-Slovaks who had originally promised him safe passage. As the White Army threatened to attack Irkutsk, the Bolsheviks were concerned that they might try to free Kolchak. The admiral was taken to a local river and executed by a Bolshevik firing squad.

This was an example of the turmoil that prevailed in these times. Admiral Kolchak was executed near Irkutsk a year after the Oganjanov family completed their 4,000 mile journey across Asia and arrived in Irkutsk.

The family must have had many adventures along the way from Armenia to Siberia, but no record of the crossing exists.

Their story begins in Irkutsk.

Chapter 23

Irkutsk Siberia

Irkutsk is a four–hundred-year-old city on the Angara River in Siberia. It lies about forty-five miles from the outflow of Lake Baikal, the deepest lake in the world, which holds nearly one quarter of all the world's fresh water. The Irkut River, which gives the city its name, joins the Angara directly across from the town. Some of the oldest landmarks in the city are the monastery and the fort that protects the town and the port. During the reign of the Tsars, Irkutsk served as an eastern branch of the Russian Empire, with a Governor General—usually a close relative of the Tsar—and politically appointed administrators to govern the province.

As a Siberian city, Irkutsk has a sub-arctic climate, with extreme variations in temperatures between seasons. Temperatures can be very warm in the summer and bitter cold in the winter. However, Lake Baikal acts like a great inland sea and moderates temperatures in Irkutsk so that the average in winter is ten below zero, milder than other parts of Siberia.

Irkutsk was established in 1652 as the winter quarters for gold and fur traders. However, in the nineteenth century, it became more cosmopolitan as many Russian writers, artists, officers and nobles were exiled to Siberia by Tsar Nicholas I. Soon Irkutsk became a major center of intellectual and social life for the exiles. By the end of the century, there were nearly as many exiles as locals in the growing city.

In 1879 the palace of the Governor General and many of the other public buildings were destroyed or ruined by a four-day fire. Three quarters of the city, including four thousand houses, were burned. However the city rebounded and was rebuilt. By 1900, with the arrival of the railroad, Irkutsk was repeatedly referred to as 'The Paris of Siberia.'

During the Civil War after the Bolshevik Revolution, Irkutsk became the center of several bloody clashes between the "Whites" and the "Reds." Admiral Kolchak's execution effectively eliminated the anti-Bolshevik resistance.

In the twentieth century the Trans-Siberian railroad made it easier to travel from Moscow to the eastern frontiers of the Russian Empire. People traveling east to places like Vladivostok on the coast would stop in the city of Irkutsk and even linger for a while.

The Flour Mill on the Island

When the Oganjanov family came to Irkutsk, Haig's father (and Nadia's grandfather) Mkrtich decided to buy a flour mill and house outside the city of Irkutsk near the village of Smolenschina. The house was situated on an island in the river. Two bridges served the island. One large bridge led to Irkutsk and a flour mill with a water-powered turbine that stood on or near the bridge. Another bridge from the house led to the village of Smolenschina. Villagers worked as servants in the house and workers in the mill.

The family was considered wealthy by virtue of the mill, which supplied flour to the city of Irkutsk. The workers would deliver the flour by horse and four wheeled wagon. Plus the family had two wheeled carts to go to the village and to the city in summer and winter.

In Siberian villages log houses were common, while in the cities the dwellings were stone, brick and wood frame construction. Mkrtich and Haig bought a large log house containing a kitchen, dining room, living room, three bedrooms, an attic, and a basement that was accessed via a trap door in the kitchen.

The brickwork was covered with plaster, and the heat was vented through pipes from iron stoves. The main stove in the kitchen was large enough for baking bread. Exposed pipes led to other rooms and provided heat throughout the house. In the winter, the temperature outside could drop to twenty below zero. There was an outhouse for a toilet. But inside the house was a bath in its own room with running water. Hot water was provided by servants after it was heated on the stove.

The Feathers in the Outhouse

The children would use a honey pot in the house that was emptied and cleaned each day, but the adults and grown children would go to the outhouse. Even elderly Gayane, the matriarch who was partially blind by this time, was helped outside.

The outhouse was a separate building set away from the house, much like the portable toilets of today. In late spring, summer and early fall, it was used like any conventional outhouse of the era. The ground was sufficiently soft for holes to be dug, and the waste produced by the family was buried. It was in the dead of winter that the "feathers" came into play.

In late fall and all through the long winter, the ground was frozen solid and—except for scraping a depression and putting a stool over it—there was nothing to do but squat and do your business on the frozen ground. However, those entering the outhouse would notice a collection of feathers hanging from the walls within easy reach. It is lost to history as to what kind of bird's feathers these were, suffice it to say, they needed to be substantial. A safe assumption might be that they were the long feathers of chickens or capons—maybe even geese slaughtered for the dinner table—and collected by the house servants. Nevertheless a supply of feathers was always available in the outhouse.

After they were done with their personal toilet, the excrement (or 'fooph' as the children called it) was still body temperature on the ground, and one more chore remained. They took a feather from the wall, moved the stool and inserted the pointy end of the feather into the pile. The pile would freeze very quickly. When the next family member came to do their business, they could safely pick up the frozen pile by the feather and toss it into a designated area in the field, as far from the house as possible.

It was one of the sad duties of the servants to go out to the field in early spring with a rake and "harvest the crop of feathers." The mature fertilizer could be rolled into the soil or moved to another location.

In later years, Nadia told this story and referred to the field of feathers as "foophsicles," a phrase that only works in English.

Haiganoush and Her Suitor (1920)

Since this household was considered the estate of a wealthy family, it was not surprising that Mkrtich's five daughters were sought after in marriage. The youngest daughter, Haiganoush, resisted because she wanted to go to school to become a professional woman. Of the other daughters, Syranoush married a shoemaker, Arousyak a baker and Betheme a man named Vartan from Irkutsk.

The fifth daughter, Shohokat, was engaged and still living with her parents.

However, when Haiganoush was eighteen years old, she became the center of attention in the family. The family had settled into their home estate on the island and the men were running their flour mill business successfully in Irkutsk. Three of the sisters had already married and moved out of the house. Haiganoush was graduating from school and was headed to the university.

So it came as a surprise when Mkrtich, her father, announced that he had arranged for her to marry a man she had never met and who did not even live nearby. Her father told her that she would be moving to Manchuria.

Apparently a businessman named Aroutium had immigrated to a Russian village named Manzhouli (or Man-chu-li) near the border of Manchuria and Siberia. He had a thriving business there and frequently traveled back and forth across the frontier conducting trade. His only regret was that he had not been successful in finding an Armenian woman to marry.

A friend of Aroutium's who had recently been a guest at the Oganjanov house said, "Wait a minute! There is a man in Irkutsk, an Armenian who has five daughters. If you go there and talk to him, perhaps you will find that one of his daughters suits you."

Aroutium took the next train to Irkutsk and found Mkrtich.

"Sir, I understand you have five daughters of marrying age," he said.

"Three of my daughters have already married and left the house. One is engaged. But my Haiganoush just finished schooling and she may be available," answered Mkrtich.

So arrangements were made and Aroutium was to arrive at the house to meet Haiganoush. At first, she wanted nothing to do with the arrangement; she was determined to go to the university and was visibly upset. Her father insisted that she meet the man and keep an open mind. Perhaps she would like the look of him. Not wishing to disappoint her father, Haiganoush agreed to meet the suitor.

Aroutium arrived to greet the family. He was tall, dark, slim, and handsome, with dark eyes and a charming manner. Immediately he realized that Haiganoush was upset. She wanted to continue her education, was not prepared to leave her family, and had only agreed to meet him so as not to disobey her father. Aroutium quickly decided to leave the decision completely in her hands.

Kneeling down before her, Aroutium presented her with a diamond watch and a diamond bracelet and said, "These are my gifts to you for even considering me as a husband. And if you decide that my marriage proposal is acceptable, you will have this as well." He showed her a diamond engagement ring.

She considered the gifts and the attractive man before her. Her family sat quietly in the other room while she made up her mind. *After all*, she thought, *I can always continue my education later*. In the end, she must have found the situation quite appealing and decided to let him continue to persuade her. The courtship must have gone well, for they married a few months after and she moved to his home and business in Manzhouli.

The story of Haiganoush was told by her daughter, Talia, who lives in Brazil with her family. Talia did not know her father well since he died relatively young—when Talia was only three years old. But she spoke fondly of the man who traveled from China to Siberia to win a young woman's heart. After Aroutium died, Haiganoush continued the family business and raised her family. The story of Haiganoush and the business in Manzhouli would figure prominently in another story of the family.

Meanwhile, back in Irkutsk, the Ohanjanov family and the mill they owned prospered. Unlike the stories of so many other Armenians, which were fraught with personal tragedy, this was one of relative good fortune.

The mill supplied flour to the city and surrounding areas. It employed a number of workers from the village and was well regarded by the neighbors. The family had no plans to go to China anytime soon and had given up on the dream of immigrating to America.

They were waiting for the revolution to pass. It was 1923 and Lenin was gathering political control over most of Asia. Haig and Arpenik had a toddler son, Aram, and their two daughters were now five and seven. Haig's sisters were married or engaged. As wealthy Bourgeois, they were occasionally harassed by the local Communists and Socialists who hated anyone with wealth, but nothing of consequence had happened.

That is, until 1923, when the murders and the robbery overwhelmed the family; then everything changed.

Chapter 24

The Murders at the Estate (1923)

To understand the circumstances of the murders and the robbery committed in 1923 a few facts must first be conveyed. It is apparent that the robbery at the estate was well planned, but it is also apparent that information from someone close to the family was necessary for the plan to succeed.

The estate was isolated on an island with two bridges. One bridge led to a nearby village Smolenshchina, while the second larger bridge led to Irkutsk. On the day of the robbery, there were several weddings at the nearby village of Smolenshchina. The villagers were all engaged in revelry and celebration. It was not uncommon for someone to fire a gun or hunting rifle during the parties, so an occasional gunshot was not unexpected. These wedding parties could go on all day and hide any other commotion.

The attack was planned for a Sunday. This was significant. The family did not go to church on Sunday because there was no Armenian Apostolic Church in Irkutsk. For special holidays, they would occasionally go to the Russian church since everyone spoke both Armenian and Russian.

Sunday was usually a quiet day at home. Also, Sunday was normally the servants' day off, so there were fewer people in the house and no workers at the mill.

Mkrtich had been harassed by the local Communists and so had hired a man to guard the property. The man would regularly walk the property in the evening and bang on the side of the house as a signal that all was normal. As long as the family heard the guard banging on the walls every hour, they felt safe.

Mkrtich had paid this man to walk around his property every day and warn the family if he saw anyone or anything suspicious. During the investigation that took place after the tragedy it was obvious that the robbers had bribed the guard to continue to reassure the family and give the impression that everything was fine. The family suspected nothing, even while the robbers were gathering outside the estate planning to break in. As soon as shots were fired, the guard ran away.

Mkrtich was sixty years old but still a vigorous patriarch. His son Haig was an Army veteran and lived in the house with his wife and two young daughters. Gayane, the matriarch, was almost totally blind by this time in her life. She was always under the care of the young grandchildren and her daughter-in-law, Arpenik. In addition, Gayane's daughter Shohokat, still living at home, watched over her mother, who sat on a sofa knitting in the living room most of the day. Nadia was playing in the house. She was five years old and remembered how the house was invaded.

The Spider Gang

In 1923, a group of robber-bandits called the Spider Gang was operating in Irkutsk. The local authorities were familiar with the gang's criminal patterns. Wearing masks that looked like black spider webs on their faces, they would invade the homes of the wealthy and steal everything available. Then they would threaten their victims to find out where they had hidden their treasure.

The family was not expecting any visitors, but Shohokat's fiancé would frequently stop by for an unexpected visit.

They were not surprised at the knock on the front door. The youngest daughter ran to the door and unlocked it without asking who was there. About fifteen people wearing masks rushed into the house.

When the bandits broke into the Oganjanov house, Mkrtich grabbed a broom and began to swing it wildly at the intruders. He was immediately shot and killed by one of the bandits. Meanwhile his wife Gayane Eckmalian began screaming uncontrollably from the living room. The bandits silenced her by shooting her as she sat on the sofa. They also shot Haig in the head as he rushed and struggled with them.

Nadia remembered seeing her father and grandfather lying on the floor, covered in blood. Her grandmother was covered with a sheet on the sofa. One of the bandits took time to play with the little girl to distract her from the grisly scene. They tossed her in the air and bounced her on their knees to keep her from getting upset.

But Nadia began to cry anyway—not because of the shots, or the noise, or the confusion—but because she wanted to pee so badly and didn't want to wet her pants. Only recently had she been fully potty trained. There was a copper pot in the kitchen, and one of the bandits put it on the floor, telling her to use it.

Now in Siberia in the winter the ground is almost entirely frozen. And the bandits knew that wealthy families often buried some of their treasure on their property. So they dragged Arpenik outside and forced her to point to where the family treasure was buried. Haig's father Mkrtich did not trust the banks in the city, since they were all run by Communists, and so he filled large cans with the family wealth and buried it on the property. However, he had not told anyone where the cans were buried. Arpenik begged the bandits to let her tend to her bleeding husband and continued to insist that she did not know where anything was buried.

They dragged Haig, who was seriously wounded, out into the yard and told his wife that if she didn't tell them where all the treasure was hidden, they would kill him.

It was then that Arpenik remembered she had seen her father-in-law digging near a large tree on the property. She took the bandits to the tree and pointed to the spot where she thought the treasure was buried.

But the ground was so frozen it was impossible to recover. They took everyone back into the house. One of the bandits picked up a revolver and said, "If we cannot get the jewels then we will have to shoot your husband." He began to count, thinking that maybe some of the treasure was still hidden in the house. Arpenik begged him to stop and insisted that she knew nothing more. Suddenly another one of the bandits came running in and said "Okay, okay, we found the can and the jewels." There may have been other cans buried on the property, but the bandits were satisfied with what they had found. It was only a matter of seconds between life and death for Haig.

The bandits knew the layout of the house and property. Someone had informed them of what was available on the estate. They took the horses and the large wagon and filled it with all the furniture, all the bedding, silverware and anything else they could load. They took all the silver and gold that they had found buried in the yard and, as darkness fell, prepared to leave.

There were several weddings in the village that day which had lasted into the night with a great deal of singing, music and dancing. So, nobody paid attention to the shots or the screaming from the house on the river nearby.

Most houses in Siberia had a cellar or basement. This one had a large basement and root cellar where potatoes, beets, vegetables and fruits were stored. Access to the cellar was gained through a trap door in the kitchen.

The family was forced down into the cellar. The trap door was blocked and several lit kerosene lamps were put on top of the door. If anyone pushed on the trap door, the kerosene lamps would tip over and the house would catch on fire.

Then the bandits fled into the night.

The Aftermath

Fortunately there was an opening from the root cellar to the outside, and everyone started yelling. Some of the people coming from the weddings in the village were crossing the bridge and heard the screams from the house. They opened the cellar door and found the trapped family, including Haig, who was badly wounded but still alive.

The police came and took everyone into Irkutsk in an automobile. Ironically, this was the first time Nadia had ridden in a car.

For the rest of her life she remembered the masked bandits who had bounced her on their knees, tossed her in the air to make her laugh, and played with her, while her parents and grandparents were being assaulted and her family robbed.

Haig recovered from his bullet wound, although he would never hear from his right ear again. Determined to find every one of the bandits, he told the police that he wanted to help in any way possible. The police were very helpful and even gave him a gun to protect his family from further incursions. Because the bandits had known so much about the security of the house— where to look for treasure and how many people would be home that night— Haig was certain that someone very close to the family was part of the gang.

He kept an eye out for suspicious behavior on the part of workers and friends. He also took regular trips to Irkutsk to ask questions and search for clues about the Spider Gang.

Sometime later, his wife Arpenik spotted a pair of earrings being worn by a woman at the market. She recognized the earrings as part of the stolen goods and quickly told her husband.

It turned out that the woman was part of the gang. Haig kept track of her until she led him to several others. He contacted the police and the gang was arrested, convicted and executed for murder.

One of the gang members turned out to be an Armenian who had visited the family on several occasions. He was the one who had told the Spider Gang that this would be a profitable house to rob.

They recovered very few of the family possessions, which had been distributed amongst the bandits and either pawned or sold.

Chapter 25

The Communists in Siberia

Haig rebuilt his business over the next five years. A second son, Grikor, was born into the family in 1924. A third son, Nicholas, was born in 1926. Nadia was now a pre-adolescent. Despite the recent tragedy, she remembered these times on the mill estate as happy. She had grown into a self reliant little girl who enjoyed exploring and hiking in the local hills with friends. She was precocious and began reading at an early age, finishing the *Arabian Nights* before she was ten. Her fascination with tales of fantasy and adventure led her to specific authors—Jules Verne, Dumas, Hugo and then later the Russian authors, particularly Gogol.

Her constant companion around the estate was a Russian wolfhound that was obtained to help protect the house. It was a huge, shaggy white beast that Nadia could ride like a pony whenever he would stand still to be mounted. Between reading, hiking and playing with the giant dog, Nadia was content with life at the mill.

However, when her youngest brother Grikor became a toddler, the dog visibly transferred all his affection. The dog would stay at Grikor's side all day long, to the exclusion of anyone else. At first Nadia was upset with the change in the dog's behavior but soon moved on to other interests. The toddler and the dog became inseparable; the family had never seen such devotion. So it was particularly tragic when Grikor became sick.

Grikor contracted a childhood disease and began to weaken rapidly. The dog stayed at his bedside and could only be removed with great effort, returning to the boy's room at every opportunity. The dog somehow knew that something was terribly wrong with the boy. Then Grikor died, and the dog sunk into what can only be described as a deep depression. The wolfhound lay on the little boy's trundle bed, moaning for his playmate.

Soon after Grikor's death, the dog was discovered at the grave, also dead. The toddler and the giant dog had been inseparable to the end.

Shortly after Grikor's death, the flour mill and house were confiscated by the Communists as state property. In 1923, while Lenin was still alive and in control of the country, free enterprise had been allowed. Lenin realized that even in a Socialistic State the people worked harder for their own goods and property than as laborers for the State. But when Lenin died and Stalin took over in 1928, all businesses were confiscated, even the independent farms. The Communists offered Haig an opportunity to stay on at his own mill as a worker. He refused.

Haig still had some money and the family moved into Irkutsk. All his life, Haig had been an independent businessman. The idea of working for others was unacceptable. He decided to try one more time to open his own business and live within the restrictions of the Communist regime. He opened a hardware store, but the Communists imposed such huge penalties, harassing regulations and taxes on anyone who owned anything that it was impossible to prosper as a businessman. Haig began to make plans to move again.

Chapter 26

The Journey to Manchuria

When Stalin took over Russia he announced that you cannot have free enterprise in a true Marxist/Leninist society. All privately owned businesses were confiscated. The long journey across Asia and the hardships the family had endured had ultimately not paid off, for the Communist Revolution had followed them into Siberia. It was at this time Haig decided to migrate into China. The plan was to position one parent in Siberia and the other in Manchuria, then bring each family member across, one by one.

The borders were closed and guarded, but Haig had heard many tales of how people had successfully made the dangerous crossing into China. He also heard what happened to people who got picked up by the border police for trying to cross without permission. They were rarely seen again. The crossing was more dangerous than ever, because the Communist border guards were ordered to stop anyone on the border and they did not hesitate to shoot those who ran. The rail line from the town of Zabaykalsk—a few miles inside Siberia—crossed into Manchuria and stopped in the town of Manzhouli on the other side. This was the only reasonable way to cross the border in the region. The guards boarded the train at Zabaykalsk and checked everyone's papers carefully to make sure they had permission to cross. At this time, they did not care who was coming into Siberia from Manzhouli, only who was trying to leave.

One tale that was told to Haig intrigued him. Apparently a clever fellow had discovered that the train coming to Zabaykalsk slowed down regularly to a crawl on a sharp turn somewhere on the frontier outside of the town. He reasoned that he could run alongside the train and hop on board. The trains leaving Russia were watched at this junction, but the trains coming into

Russia had been checked in Manzhouli and would be checked again only after they arrived in Zabaykalsk. This idea might sound foolish, because the fellow had hopped on a train that was coming into Communist Russia, not leaving.

The fellow's plan required elaborate acting. He made sure he had no identification and that his clothes and appearance identified him as a vagrant who had had too much to drink and had somehow climbed aboard the train somewhere in Manchuria and fallen asleep undetected.

Apparently he was quite the actor. He convinced the people on board who found him that he was out of his mind and an idiot to boot. He pretended that he could not speak except in grunts and Chinese curses and he acted drunk and confused to the point of belligerence. By the time the train pulled into Zabaykalsk, the authorities were called and everyone was upset and complaining about this incoherent bum, who was wreaking havoc, smelled awful and behaved like a lunatic.

The authorities could find nothing to indicate where he was from and were not interested in providing food, clothing and shelter to an obvious Manchurian vagrant. So they chained him up in the freight car of the next train and sent him across the border to plague the people in Manzhouli. He had successfully escaped by being undesirable.

Haig considered the story and decided this was never going to work for him. The guards were not going to be fooled more than once and besides, Haig was not that good an actor. He decided on a more straightforward escape plot.

The Amur River separates Siberia from China and has always been a favorite winter crossing. It is three miles wide in some areas and totally frozen in winter. During the winter, when the river froze, migrating nomads had for centuries been able to walk across. One of the tributaries of the Amur was the Argun River, which defines the border between Siberia and Manchuria.

Haig made the crossing of the Argun in winter at night by foot. He had found an isolated spot on a moonless night and began to run across as quietly as possible. But the border guards who patrolled the region must have been alerted. They put lights on the river and began to shoot at anything that moved. Although the border guards were firing at him to stop, he ran across and hid in the thickets along the bank until they gave up looking for him. He bragged later that the bullets came so close he found bullet holes in the hem of the large army coat he was wearing.

After crossing the border into Manchuria, Haig made his way to Manzhouli, where his sister had a grocery and general store in town. Haiganoush took him in, and they began to make preparations to smuggle the children from Irkutsk.

Arpenik, who had stayed behind with the children, had sufficient funds to make the necessary arrangements.

Haig had Greek friends who were import-exporters with visas that allowed them to cross the border on business. They made arrangements to 'adopt' the three children—Isabella, Nadia, and the toddler Nicky—and list them in the exit paperwork. The next time the Greeks went to China they bribed some guards not to look too closely at the children or ask too many questions. This was how the children got across the border. The Greeks then delivered the children to Haig in Manzhouli.

Aram was about eight years old at the time and for some reason needed to cross separately. In order to get him across the border safely on the train, they put him in a large basket and paid a conductor to put the basket on the upper bunk and cover it with a blanket. They had kept Aram awake for a day and a half, so he was sound asleep in the overhead when the guards came by. When the train finally arrived across the border, Aram was met by his Aunt Haiganoush and reunited with his father.

Arpenik's Border Crossing

The children had been successfully smuggled out of Irkutsk into Manchuria. Only Arpenik was left to cross alone, and it was now early spring in Siberia.

Haig had hired a Chinese guide who spoke Russian to bring her across the border. The guide and his assistants were to accompany Arpenik across the frontier and bring her to Manzhouli. During the night, while stopping to rest and search for a good spot to cross the river, they began to smoke opium and drink.

Arpenik became frightened for her safety and ran away from the guide. They were laughing and yelling for her to come out of hiding, but she was sure they were dangerous and left the trail and began to wander in the wilderness.

She suddenly found herself all alone with no food, water or provisions in the frontier between Siberia and Manchuria. Her only protection against the elements was a large coat. The coat was valuable for more than its warmth; she had sewn several pieces of jewelry inside the lining.

Haig and Arpenik had also taken gold pieces, painted them black, and turned into large buttons to replace the coat's original buttons. If she lost all her money, this gold would pay for the border crossing.

Now separated from her guide, she had no idea which way to go.

The Wall of Genghis Khan

The most likely route when traveling from Irkutsk to the frontier border between Siberia and Manchuria would be by rail. The China Far East Railway was completed in 1901 in accordance with the Sino-Russian Secret Treaty of 1896. This railway was the link that connected Siberia to Manchuria and ran from Irkutsk to Harbin in Northern China. The border was about halfway between these two major cities. The train had carried Arpenik from Irkutsk to the border town of Zabaykalsk, a few miles from the border crossing.

The border that separates Siberia from Manchuria is defined by the Argun River, a major tributary of the Amur. The Chinese sometimes called the Amur the Black River or the Black Dragon. Today a tourist traveling up the Amur will find Russia on one bank and China on the other. Travelers up the river encounter the several tributaries (Argun and Shilka Rivers) in Manchuria that form the Amur. From Northern China, the Amur runs 1,000 miles east to the ocean near the island of Sakhalin.

The Argun is the Russian name of the river in the region near Manzhouli. This was where the Chinese guides took Arpenik to cross. It was established as the Russo-Chinese border by the Treaty of Nerchinsk in 1689. Also crossing this region is the Wall of Genghis Khan, which extends many miles from Mongolia reaching into Northern China. The Wall of Genghis Khan passes between the Russian town of Zabaykalsk and the Manchurian town of Manzhouli. It is undoubtedly a landmark that Arpenik would have seen as she traveled in the region.

Genghis Khan united the nomadic tribes of Mongolia and northeast Asia and conquered the known world from Northern China to Eastern Europe, including the Caucasus before he died in 1227. Some scholars speculate that if he and several of his key generals had not died during his last westward campaign, he might have conquered most of Europe as well. His grandson Kublai Khan completed the conquest of China and united that country under his rule as emperor. Kublai Khan became a central figure in the stories of Marco Polo.

The Wall of Genghis Khan—unlike the Great Wall in China, which is made of brick and stone—is an earthen mound created to slow invaders from Russia and China into Mongolia. In some places it is thirty feet high, while elsewhere it is just a mound of dirt worn down by erosion and travel. It was not built by Genghis Khan since it dates almost 300 years before his birth. But the wall carries his name because of his fame in the region.

When Arpenik arrived by rail in Zabaykalsk with the Chinese guide and his assistants, they had to disembark because they did not have permission to cross into China. It was at this point that Arpenik was frightened by her guides and became lost in the wilderness.

The guide and his assistants soon gave up trying to find her, possibly thinking she would eventually get hungry and return to the border town of Zabaykalsk. They were sure that she would not swim across the Argun without help. But Arpenik was determined to cross into China and reunite with her children and husband. She found the river and walked along its banks, looking for a place to cross.

There she was spotted by a border patrol, who took her prisoner and delivered her to the captain of the police at the nearest outpost. The outpost had a station for the border staff and a guarded bridge across the Argun.

Captured by the Border Police

"What are you doing here?" The police captain demanded, "Why are you stumbling around out here in the wilderness all alone?"

Arpenik was silent, trying desperately to decide what to say. When she didn't answer, he offered "Did you get lost?" When she shrugged, he gave a puzzled look to the guard who had brought her in. Maybe she wasn't in her right mind, he thought.

Arpenik knew that her fate lay in the hands of these policemen. People picked up by the border police, if suspected of spying or criminal behavior, sometimes disappeared into the prison system and were never heard from again.

She looked at the captain for a few moments and then finally decided to speak plainly, "My children are on the other side of the river in Manzhouli. I need to find them."

The captain laughed and thought she surely must be lightheaded and confused.

"Look, I will tell the authorities in Irkutsk that you just got lost." He turned to the guard and said, "Take her back to town and have a policeman escort her on the train so she can return to Irkutsk."

The captain returned to his paperwork but Arpenik did not move. "I will go quietly but I will not stay in Irkutsk," she insisted. "If you put me on the train, I will simply take the next train here and come back again. My children are on the other side of the river, and I must find them."

"Perhaps you don't realize how serious this is," the captain said with some anger in his voice and very little patience. "You have broken the law; you could be put in jail for trying to cross the border without permission. You know that trying to cross without the proper authorization is illegal, don't you? I am going to have to send you back to Irkutsk. If you don't stop talking nonsense, the authorities there may decide to put you in jail. Now do you understand? Would you prefer to go to jail?"

Arpenik looked at the police captain and answered quietly, "If you put me on the train I will come back. If you put me in jail, I will sit quietly until the day you no longer want to keep me in jail. And then I will come back."

She leaned forward and never took her eyes off the police captain. "I will keep coming back here because my family is on the other side of the river and I must find them. I will keep coming back until I find my children. You must understand. I will not live without them." She hesitated and then added, "Please, please let me go."

Arpenik was sure they would soon search her and discover the gold buttons. So she tried one last appeal. She ripped several of the gold buttons from her coat and placed them on the desk before the captain. "You can take everything I own, my earrings, anything of value, these buttons, everything, but let me go find my family," she pleaded.

The captain looked at the woman and picked up the buttons she had laid before him. He scraped paint until he could see the gold.

Now it's not clear what happened next. Perhaps the gold and jewelry influenced him, though he could have taken them and still put her in jail. Or maybe all this was too much bother, too much paperwork over some lightheaded woman lost at the border. Or maybe he just felt admiration for this small woman with a strong spirit—maybe even sympathy for her. No one is sure what motivated him, but clearly he and the guard were moved by her determination. Maybe he just wanted to be part of an effort to reunite a desperate mother with her children. No one really knows why the police captain did what he did.

Whatever the reason, there was silence for a few moments and then the captain turned to the guard, and said, "Take this mother to the bridge and let her cross. See that she gets safely to the other side."

The guard escorted Arpenik to the bridge while several other guards watched. He motioned for her to walk across.

"I cannot give you anything for your journey, not even water. I will get into trouble if I help you," said the guard. "Stay on the dirt path when you reach the other side and do not fall asleep in the woods—there are wolves and bears there. It is a long way to the nearest town, but keep moving away from the river."

Arpenik was unsure of her good fortune. Perhaps the guards might shoot her when she crossed the river. After all, the guards had instructions to shoot anyone trying to escape to China. Her husband had nearly been killed by border guards running across this same river in the winter earlier that year. They might even have been the same guards.

Halfway across the bridge, she gathered her courage and turned to look back. The guards were talking among themselves and waving to her. They motioned for her to keep going.

When she reached the other side, she waved back to them and began the long walk to Manzhouli. She was now in Manchuria, miles from civilization, back in the wilderness.

Chapter 27

Manzhouli

The town of Manzhouli is located on the Hulunbuir grasslands. Lake Hulun to its immediate south is China's fifth largest freshwater lake, with an area of 2,600 square kilometers and an average depth of just five meters.

In ancient times this area was inhabited by many tribes who lived in Manchuria, including the Donghu, the Xiongnu, the Xianbei, the Khitan, the Jurchen, and the Mongols. From the early Qing Dynasty onwards the Argun River, which originates in this area, became the border between the Manchu Empire and Russia. Russia is directly to the north, and it shares a border fifty-four kilometers long. Zabaykalsk, situated immediately north of the Abagaitu Islet and Manzhouli, is the nearest Russian town.

Soon after the China Far East Railway was complete, a settlement was formed around Manchzhuriya Station, the first stop in Manchuria for Russians entering Northern China. That station was the beginning of the modern town of Manzhouli, a name derived from the Russian Manchzhuriya.

Manzhouli was designated a trading center in the Sino-Japanese Treaty of 1905, greatly boosting Manzhouli's growth. The Manzhouli customs was set up in 1908. Under the Republic of China, Manzhouli came under the jurisdiction of the province of Hsingan. After the Japanese army occupied the surrounding area in 1931, Manzhouli actually came under Japanese control and was part of the Empire of Manchukuo from 1932 until the end of World War II in 1945.

Many Russian émigrés settled in the town after the Bolshevik revolution. From 1913 until 1949, when the region became the NE Inner Mongolian Autonomous Region of China, the town was also known as Lubin.

Winters in Manzhouli are as treacherous as one might expect a town sitting on the southern fringes of Siberia to be. It is dry and cold enough to freeze all moisture into a thick sheet of opaque ice on the outer buffer zone of the windows that don't get direct sunlight in a house. The light coming in these windows is always obscured and the glass looks like the bottom of a poorly manufactured bottle.

Because it is so dry, the entire winter can pass without snow. In this part of the world, it snows only in late fall and early spring.

It was early spring when Arpenik made her journey on foot from the Zabaykalsk border crossing to Manzhouli. There may actually have been snow on the ground. But it most certainly was not the deep winter, as it had been when Haig ran across the frozen river.

During winter, air moisture freezes into glittering airborne miniature blades that slash windpipes and freeze lungs with every breath. It reaches a minimum of minus forty degrees Celsius (the same in Fahrenheit, minus forty). Travelers without hats would freeze their ears, and the exposed frozen skin would flake off for weeks.

As a child, Nadia made the mistake of going outside without gloves and grabbing a cast iron water pump handle to see if she could get a drink. Her hand immediately froze to the handle and she began screaming in pain.

When the adults came out in response to her screams, they realized immediately that if they tried to remove her hand from the pump handle, her frozen skin would come off on the metal. Her father disconnected the pump handle and brought the girl and the mechanism indoors to slowly heat up her hand before frostbite set in. Even so, her hand was blistered for weeks. But she was spared the pain of blackened fingers.

Anyone who lost their gloves in this climate and had exposed fingers for any duration risked a serious case of frostbite. The fingers would swell and blacken, the tips would need to be surgically removed and the pain in the joints would never go away.

In this kind of harsh environment, beer and milk are always served at room temperature. To chill liquids, the strategy is to put the bottles outside for ten or fifteen minutes and watch so that they don't freeze over. Milk left at the door by a delivery service must be brought inside immediately. Otherwise it will expand over the top of the bottle and form a cream cap that the children love to eat like ice cream. Then you are left with skim milk.

After the long winter, Haig and his children were safe with his sister, Haiganoush. Haiganoush had come to Manzhouli years earlier to marry and raise a family. Her husband had died young and left her to care for two young children, Talia and Alik. But he also left a grocery and general store that provided a living and an apartment in the same building.

Haig was now running the business while his sister cared for the children.

The store in Manzhouli was in the heart of the town and included a grocery, general store and butcher shop with a sign that identified the owners as 'Oganjanov.' This was the Russianized version of the Armenian name, Ohanjanian. The store was in a multi-storied building.

The family lived in the apartments upstairs, and the front of the store and the upstairs kitchen faced the street.

Together Haig and Haiganoush ran the business and took care of the sister's two children and the brother's four. Nadia was now eleven years old.

Everyone in the family was concerned about the disappearance of Arpenik. Haig had received a telegram several days earlier from a friend in Irkutsk. Arpenik had left Irkutsk but had been separated from her guide and disappeared into the wilderness near Zabaykalsk. She had probably been picked up by the Soviet police.

All their careful plans were in disarray. Haig was unsure what to do. It would be impossible to find her without help. And he was now in Manchuria. How could he help from here?

If she had been picked up by the border police, she was lost to them. The family knew that anyone in Soviet police custody for trying to cross the border would be in jail. The police were notorious for never answering questions about prisoners.

Haig could only hope that she had made her way back to Zabaykalsk on the Siberia side of the river and would contact him. Then they could try to get her across some other way.

While Haig waited for news, he kept his mind busy by focusing on the business. Every morning he would rise early and start the day with a large breakfast. He usually ate one meal for the day consisting of six eggs and a slab of bacon. Each morning before opening the doors, he'd spend time organizing the produce, gathering scraps from the butcher section and identifying stale bread and vegetables.

The scraps and bread were for the beggar women who regularly came to the store to get whatever was available. These were widows without means or women who had been abandoned by family. Haig was generous in helping the beggars, who had no other means to sustain themselves. So it was no surprise to hear a commotion downstairs in the street in front of the store.

He quickly looked out the second story window and saw a beggar woman covered in dirt in front of the store. She could barely speak as she stood in the street and knocked on the door.

"Okay, you can wait; I am coming down after breakfast. I am not ready for you," he yelled down to her. "We are not open". He returned to his breakfast. By now, Haiganoush and Nadia were up and about. They also heard the knocking on the front door.

"The beggars have come early this morning," Haig said to his sister.

From below, Arpenik thought that Haig was talking to her and telling her to come back later. She said in Armenian, "It is me. Do you not know me?"

Nadia ran to the window and said, "It is Mommy". Everyone ran downstairs to open the door and bring the exhausted mother inside. They placed her on the sofa and began to attend to her, all the while crying with joy and relief.

Apparently, after the police released her, she had spent a day and night in the wilderness, not daring to sleep or even rest. Her face was almost unrecognizable, because it had become swollen and covered with blisters from exposure. She was covered in dirt and thorns from stumbling through the tall grass and taiga.

She had not been sure which way to go other than away from the river. Late at night she was fortunate to see a faint glow on the horizon that identified the general direction of the town. She had walked into the town at dawn that morning and immediately began to look for any sign of her family. Because it was so early there was no one about. The town was quite large but somehow she had managed to find the store with the family name on it.

As the family gathered around her, Nicky, her youngest child, was heard to say, "But I don't want this mommy, I want my real mommy." It took some time to convince him that the beggar woman with the swollen face was indeed his real mother.

Years later, when this story was told and retold, Arpenik would remind her husband how badly he had behaved when he first saw her in the street.

"Always remember," she joked, "I am a melik and you are a simple merchant. You must always open the door for a melik."

Chapter 28

The Family Moves to Harbin

While Arpenik was recovering from her ordeal on the frontier, the family took stock of their situation. Haiganoush was a widow with two young children, and the business in Manzhouli could not support two families. Haiganoush decided to move to Harbin with her children. She married soon after that, went back to school and settled into her new life as a Harbinite.

Meanwhile her brother, who had reunited with his family, handled the business in Manchuria and began to make plans of his own. Manzhouli was obviously not the place to be; the city with the largest Russian population outside of Russia was located farther into Northern China; it was the frozen city of Harbin.

After selling the business in Manzhouli, Haig moved his family to Harbin to start another business there. His oldest child Isabella went to the university in Harbin and graduated as a dentist. She was soon providing dental service to the region from a train that toured the countryside. Nadia finished her schooling and decided to visit her brother Aram in Shanghai. Aram, the older of the two sons, had joined the merchant marines and begun a career as a seaman.

Even under the occupation of China by the imperialistic Japanese and during an economic depression that gripped other parts of the world, the years between 1920 to 1940 in Harbin and Shanghai were prosperous. Many new businesses were started and many succeeded because credit could easily be obtained from the Chinese moneylenders. The main condition was that everything must be repaid on time; if you fell behind, you were denied any more credit.

Nadia at the rail station in Harbin

By the late 1930s Harbin was already ranked as the tenth largest city in China, serving as a key cultural, political, economic, scientific, and communications center for Northeastern China.

On a map of the Heilongjiang province, the shape of Heilongjiang resembles a swan. That is why Harbin is nicknamed, "The pearl on the swan's neck." It has also been called the "Oriental Moscow" or "Oriental Paris" for its architecture. In some references, Harbin is also known as "the Ice City" for its long, cold winter. This city has become particularly famous for its beautiful display of ice sculptures in winter.

The Ice and Snow Sculptures of Harbin

Harbin is a worldwide center for ice and snow culture. Geographically, it is located under the direct influence of the cold winter wind from Siberia. The average temperature in summer is twenty-one degrees Celsius and in winter, minus seventeen degrees Celsius. It can be as cold as minus forty degrees Celsius.

The Harbin International Ice and Snow Sculpture Festival was formally initiated in 1985, but the actual tradition started much earlier. In fact, throughout the twentieth century many sculptures were created every January to decorate the city. It has been a tradition for ice and snow lanterns to illuminate full-size buildings made from blocks of ice. Meanwhile the populace enjoys winter activities that include winter-swimming in the Songhua River and the exhibition of ice-lanterns in Zhaolin Garden. The snow carvings and ice and snow recreations in and around Harbin have now become world famous.

The ice lanterns of Harbin and Northern China have been a winter-time tradition in Northeast China for centuries. During the Qing Dynasty (1644-1911), the local peasants and fishermen often made and used ice lanterns as jack-lights during the winter months. At that time they were created simply by pouring water into a bucket that was put out in the open to freeze. They were then gently warmed before the water froze completely so that the bucket-shaped block of ice could be pulled out. A hole was chiseled in the top and the water remaining inside poured out, creating a hollow vessel. A candle was then placed inside, resulting in a windproof lantern with a shimmering light that glowed through the ice. These lanterns were very popular in the area around Harbin.

People made ice lanterns and put them outside their houses or gave them to children to play with during some of the traditional festivals. With the advancement in technique, today people can marvel at the various delicate and artistic ice lanterns on display during the Winter Festival in Harbin. The ice lanterns are an exotic addition to the marvelous sculptures seen everywhere, adding a wondrous light to the ice palaces and ice skyscrapers that decorate the city throughout the winter.

Ice and Snow Festival - Harbin, China

Chapter 29

Japanese Occupation

In the mid-1930s, the Japanese occupied Manchuria and turned it into the puppet state of Manchukuo. In 1935 the Soviet Union sold its share of the China Eastern Railway to Japan. Thousands of Harbin Russians who wanted to maintain their Russian identity boarded the trains with their passports and belongings and left for the Soviet Union. Nearly all of them were arrested during the Great Purge (1936–1938) and charged with espionage and counter-revolutionary activity. Many literally disappeared into the infamous Gulags.

From 1932 to 1945, Harbin Russians had a difficult time under the Manchukuo régime and the Japanese occupation. Some Harbin Russians initially thought the occupation was fine. They were hoping the Japanese would help them in their anti-Soviet struggles and provide protection from the Chinese, who were desperately trying to regain sovereignty over Harbin. But a substantial number moved south to Shanghai or emigrated to the United States and Australia.

The Oganjanov family lived a comfortable life in Harbin for ten years, despite the occupation. Nadia and the family left Manzhouli in 1929 when she was eleven. From 1929 to 1937, she got most of her formal education in Russian gymnasiums in Harbin, where she excelled at physics, chemistry and language.

It was now 1940, and rumors of war between Japan and America were starting to spread across Asia. At the invitation of her brother Aram, Nadia decided to visit Shanghai before travel became restrictive.

At nineteen Aram had joined the merchant marines. He had always wanted to be a seaman and see the world. He had been to Shanghai while on furlough. As a seaman he would often come to Shanghai and other port cities.

But he particularly bragged about the beauty of Shanghai. So Nadia went to see it.

Shortly after her arrival, Nadia and Aram visited the Armenian Social Club in Shanghai. Here she met George, and he immediately fell in love with her. He pursued her for two years with little success. But he was amusing, charming and persistent. When she finally agreed to his many marriage proposals, a new adventure awaited her.

Part III

THE POST WAR YEARS
1945 to 1951

Chapter 30

Working with the American Military

By late 1945, World War II was over. The Americans were now in Shanghai at the invitation of Chang Kai-shek. But times were hard. The Japanese had stolen as much as they could to support their war effort. Some people were literally starving. George and Nadia had married three years earlier. During the war years, George had worked for the Egyptian import and export trading company on the Bund. Working with him at the time was his friend Leon. George and Leon became good friends as young men when they first arrived in Shanghai. They had both lived in the Armenian Social Club prior to World War II. George stayed at the club until he married.

George and Leon had worked for Yervand Hamamdjian in the import and export company until the war ended. They were both on the Bund when the Conte Verde was scuttled in the Whangpoo River. Leon worked in Receiving and did record-keeping on the inventory, while George did bookkeeping and office work. But by the end of the war, George was married and just starting a family. When he and Leon asked for more money from their boss and he refused to raise their pay, they both left.

Soon after the arrival of the Americans, the city's economic environment improved greatly.

The Commander of the American forces, General Wedemeyer, approved the hiring of many Russians to work for the Americans at their facilities. The Americans required an enormous staff, and many people could find work and receive excellent wages. They were chauffeurs, cooks, clerks, and mechanics—everything needed for the facilities.

When they left the import export business, Leon came to George and said, "Let's go and see what jobs we can get with the Americans. I understand they want to hire all kinds of workers for the main base."

George asked, "Why are the Americans hiring foreign nationals to work on their bases?"

"So the soldiers don't have to bother. They can just sit around and drink," was the answer Leon gave.

Leon, like many good Armenians, had few scruples when it came to making money. When he found out that the Americans were hiring foreign nationals for various jobs on the military bases, he maneuvered to get a job in the PX maintaining the inventory. This put him in an ideal position to pilfer supplies from the PX and sell them on the black market.

Of course he did not consider this black marketeering, but just good Armenian entrepreneurship; he was taking proper advantage of an opportunity. At one point, he had removed enough supplies from the PX to fill several lorries with the contraband. He enlisted several friends to store the merchandise in their garages until he could sell it off.

With a wife and child to support, George began to look for more legitimate work. George was hired by the American Military Police, and that was his first contact with the Americans since his days at RCA in Dairen. He was hired as auxiliary military personnel and served as a security guard at the base. The position required a uniform and adherence to military protocol. He was not part of the American military but he might as well have been, for all the rules and regulations he needed to follow.

Because of his skill with languages, George was promoted to the rank of corporal. His duties included guarding the main gate to the American army base and dealing with multi-lingual issues. Very quickly he began to get painful lessons in American ingenuity and humor. George had always been the prankster. But now he became the victim of expert pranksters—American soldiers. He remembered one incident in particular.

One day he was standing on duty as a main guard in the American compound. Because George was a corporal and spoke English well, he was at the main gate near the office. There were guards all-around the compound and a curfew was in effect. No one was allowed to leave the base without written permission. There had been too many instances of Americans getting drunk and being picked up by the police.

So everyone was restricted to base after dark. Suddenly a lieutenant drove up in a jeep to the main gate. A captain was sitting beside the lieutenant.

The lieutenant said to George, "The captain is very sick and I have to take him to the hospital." The captain was a good actor, so gullible George thought this was an emergency and believed them. He let them out of the compound. So where do you think they went? The first thing they did was visit the first bar they came across and get drunk.

The MPs on patrol saw them and asked, "What are you doing here after curfew?" They offered no coherent answers, so the MPs grabbed the men and brought them back.

All of a sudden George saw the MP jeep coming up to the gate with these two comedians in the back. The MPs asked George "Are these boys from here? Yep. You let them out? Yep. Why?"

So George said, "The captain is very sick, and the lieutenant was taking him to the hospital."

Of course the lieutenant and the captain were sitting there laughing, "Ha, ha, ha." George had to go back to the billet, and the MPs had to make a report.

Soon after, the commanding officer, Major Rayner, called George to his office and 'sliced George like bologna' from up one side to the other for letting anybody out after curfew without written permission.

This Major was an unusual spit and polish officer, and George actually liked him. He was strict but would do anything for his men. He provided everything that was needed and fought for any and all provisions. However the major was particular about conduct and appearance. He was the kind of officer who was constantly inspecting all of your buttons. If he caught his men unshaved, or if their boots were dirty, they were in big trouble.

The Major was living in the American Club next to the base. And there was one guard post right across the street in the parking lot. He would come to the club window, get behind a curtain, and stand there watching the guards as they lit a cigarette. The guards didn't always know when he was at the American Club, so if, all of a sudden, Major Rayner found out they were smoking on duty, he would come out and go to work on them.

Unscheduled inspections were another of his specialties. He came one day to George's guard post while he was on duty. George was about to sit down when the jeep pulled up. There was Major Rayner, with a lieutenant driving. Right away he started questioning George.

"How many guards do you have on duty here? What are the duties?" He asked about this and that and everything. George answered all the questions. The Major hadn't found anything to complain about, but he kept walking around, looking for something, and talking.

After looking George over carefully, he seemed to be satisfied, but then he looked up at his cap. Part of the uniform at that time was this Eisenhower cap, which was supposed to be worn exactly one inch above your eyebrows. The Major wanted to find something out of place during this surprise inspection but he couldn't find anything wrong, because George answered all the questions and looked fine. Still, he reached up and fixed the cap—which wasn't exactly one inch above his eyebrows—and issued a demerit.

It was clear to everyone, including George, that George was not cut out to be a military guard. He was too affable, too quick to joke with the soldiers who took advantage and kept sneaking off the base. To his relief, within a few months, when the American military found out that George spoke or understood several languages besides English, they offered him another job as a translator. He was happy to leave his brief military career for an easier job helping immigrants with their visas rather than suffering any more inspections.

Even though these associations with the Americans in China were brief, they proved to be valuable connections when the time came to leave China and find a better life. They also reinforced preconceived perceptions that George had developed about Americans convincing him that America was the place for him. Each American he met was positive and confident. They enjoyed life and laughed about everything. They were all wheelers dealers with grand visions about their futures back home. They were nothing like the Europeans that George had met in Harbin and Shanghai up to now. George liked Americans almost as soon as he got to know them.

Chapter 31

The Chikan Theater

While the war years were very hard, after World War II things did get better. A year after working for the American military, George was asked to manage a large movie theater near Shanghai called the Chikan. The job would afford him the opportunity to be an independent businessman, something he had wanted for a long time. George had learned how to handle electronics, audio equipment and projectors at RCA Victor in Dairen and he had a good business sense. Also, at the Armenian Social Club he had directed several ethnic plays and theatrical productions. This was important experience.

The theaters of the late 1940s were large and had live shows on stage to introduce the movies. The entertainers were local but the productions were often quite elaborate. The Chikan Theater in Shanghai was named for a town about 200 kilometers from Shanghai. After George and Nadia were married, they lived in the large multistory apartment behind the same building.

George was the manager of the Chikan Theater for several years. There are photographs of the Chikan that show a large staff of people and a multi-story modern theatrical building that was used to play modern cinema and provide a stage for various live productions. George had become successful and the family was now comfortable. Nadia had just given birth to a second child, a daughter, and the family lived in the apartment with an amah taking care of the children.

Unfortunately it soon became apparent that the country would be taken by the Communists and Chang Kai-shek could not remain on the mainland.

浙江影院同人歡送 *MR. & MRS. G. SARGOYAN* 離滬留念 *18 12 1948*

George, Nadia and young son (center) pose for a picture with the staff of the Chikan
Theatre prior to the "great banquet"

In 1948, the generalissimo left mainland China for the islands just off the
coast. The Communists were coming and everyone was given very little time
to decide what to do. Should they stay and try to work with the new regime, or
leave with the Americans who had all but deided to abandon China?

The Last Banquet

As the Communists approached the city, George decided he and the
family must leave China with the Americans. Years later he learned from
those who stayed behind that life was awful after the Communists took over.
The value of the businesses in the International District dropped to next to
nothing. The Communists regarded all requests with suspicion and threw
up obstacles to any entrepreneurial activities, calling them subversive and
counter-revolutionary.

Before the Communists entered the city of Shanghai, George and Nadia
decided to host a banquet for the theater staff. Friends and employees were
invited for a formal dinner. A regular chef would never do for such a party, so

George hired a banquet chef who specialized in such affairs. One morning the chef ceremoniously took George to the open market to pick the ingredients for the banquet. George learned that the host of the party was expected to approve all selections.

They walked up and down the stalls, picking the plumpest worms and eels, carp fish and small birds—all alive, of course. The chef would point out the best in each open barrel or tank and George would nod knowingly at the various exotic produce available for sale. There were also aged, pickled and preserved ingredients such as chicken feet pickled in sweet sauce, blackened soy duck, pigeons, hummingbirds and beetles. Also purchased were various types of seafood and crustaceans, exotic fowl, and meats that could not be identified other than as some type of skinned mammal. Everything had to be special; nothing ordinary would do for this last banquet. When all ingredients were bought, the chef, with the help of a special staff, began to prepare the sauces and spices for each dish.

The banquet was held at very large tables that served all the guests. The various dishes were placed in a large Lazy Susan in the middle of the table. The trays revolved and presented the exquisite culinary creations to each guest. The guest used their chopsticks to add a small sample of whatever caught their eye to a bowl of steamed rice or noodles. They would typically tuck the bowl under their chins and begin to eat each sample separately before going back for the next taste treat.

The banquet chef would move around the table to interpret the guests' reactions. In many cases, the presentation was as important as the taste. The only dish that George ever described in detail was the large carp fish. It was picked live from a crystal clear fresh water tank at the market and prepared whole, covered in a crunchy orange glaze. Every part of the fish was edible, including brain and eyes—a special treat for either the guest of honor or the host. In all his travels, George never saw this fish available anywhere but from the chefs of Shanghai.

In addition, the Lazy Susan included one bowl of plain noodles per table. As the dinner progressed, the bowl of noodles was presented to each person at the table. If anyone took some plain noodles, the banquet would continue, because that was a polite signal that the guests were still hungry. And so the chef would disappear into the kitchen to supervise more dishes. This was as much a test of the chef as it was a test of the appetite of the guests. There were no duplicate dishes and each guest was encouraged to sample everything. It all needed to be perfect to earn compliments for the host.

This whole affair was also important for the kitchen staff. The chef was paid by the host and could even earn an extra reward from some of the guests who were particularly impressed with his abilities.

There was no such thing as tipping as is understood in the Western culture. Only excellence was rewarded. But the kitchen staff would traditionally divide everything left over from the banquet. That was their reward. If the host had been generous in selecting ingredients (and the banquet chef would encourage generosity) then there would be a great deal left when the banquet was over. The staff could take what was left as part of their day's wages for labor in the kitchen. But if the guests kept eating from the bowl of plain noodles, then the banquet would have to continue, leaving less and less for the staff to divide.

As the evening progressed and the banquet continued, each time the bowl of noodles was ceremoniously passed to the guests, some of the staff would peek in from the kitchen and report back. Each time someone took more noodles, the banquet continued and the staff got busy preparing more food and expecting less reward. Finally the bowl came around and each guest made it clear that they were finished by waving it aside and belching loud and clear.

The belch was also a cultural tradition that complimented the host on how satisfied the diner was with the meal.

A loud long belch followed by a verbal salute of "Chabolla" was greeted by everyone with laughter and applause. The verbal salute told the host that the banquet was a success and the vocal guest in question was well satisfied. When the last guest had refused the bowl, the banquet was over and a signal was given to the staff to clear the table and divide the leftovers.

This would be the last time that George and Nadia would see many of their friends and employees. While everyone laughed and claimed that the current political crisis was only temporary, most of them knew that the end was near. Everything was about to change in Shanghai.

Chapter 32

A Long Road to America

In late 1945, when the war was over with Japan, the Chinese Communist Red Army started advancing on Chang Kai-shek and the Nationalist positions. The Red Army advanced upon the Nationalists in Northern China and forced many emigrants living in Hankow, Peking, Tientsin, Tsingtao, and elsewhere to move to Shanghai. Eventually the Communists occupied most of the major cities and Chang Kai-shek retreated to Changking. Chang Kai-shek and his wife pleaded with the United Nations and the American administration to intercede. So much was happening so quickly that there was a great deal of chaos and confusion. The American military was still occupying some sections of the country. The United Nations' International Refugee Organization, IRO, recognized that many refugees were undocumented but still tried to arrange to move them out of China, while the Nationalists and the Communists were trying to consolidate control of key areas of strategic importance. No one knew who was in charge.

The political unrest at the time was a direct result of a lack of central leadership, a vacuum left by the war. China had been ruled for centuries by an Emperor in Peking and a whole conglomeration of war lords who controlled local districts. When the Japanese invaded China in the 1930s, they captured the Emperor, Henry Pu Yi, and put him in charge of Manchuria in a puppet government. Meanwhile the Japanese left the rest of the country to the war lords, controlling the coastal cities.

Chang Kai-shek was the first general to unite many of the districts and form a national army. The Nationalists mainly fought Communists and rebels. But in the 1920s a popular bandit, political leader and agitator named Mao Tse-Tung was funded by the Communists in Russia to create unrest in China and possibly topple the Nationalists. When the Japanese invaded China, Chang Kai-shek formed an alliance with Mao, who was living in caves in the mountains of central China. They agreed to fight the Japanese together. But, even during the Japanese occupation, Mao was secretly forming a rebellion against the Nationalists.

Chang Kai-shek became an ally of the Americans when war broke out between the U.S. and Japan in 1941. The Americans kept coming across the Pacific or flying over the Himalayas to attack Japanese positions. Meanwhile Chang Kai-shek tried to drive the Japanese from the mainland and the Japanese, except for a few coastal cities, finally abandoned China to go back to Japan to defend the motherland. At the same time Mao was leading the peasants living in the mountains and conducting guerrilla warfare against the Japanese.

Near the end of World War II Chang Kai-shek became head of the Nationalist Party and President of China. America sent warships to coastal China and helped the Chinese drive the Japanese out of the cities.

But the alliance between the Nationalists and the Communists proved false. The Communist plan was to let Chang Kai-shek and the Japanese just battle it out. When the Japanese surrendered in 1945, Mao attacked the Nationalists. By 1948, Mao had driven Chang Kai-shek out of China to establish his government on Formosa. Mao then was able to take over the remainder of China.

The Communists encouraged hatred for all foreigners because of perceived oppression by Europeans during long years of occupation in China. When the fighting ended and the Communists took over the country, they gave the occidentals ultimatums. The foreigners could remain under Communist directives but turn over all businesses they owned to the State, or sell the businesses, pay a fee and flee the country.

The Chaos during Evacuation

During this time one of the Chinese gendarmerie officers and his family who were retreating from Communist advances came to George's apartment. The officer just walked in and settled down. At the first opportunity, George called the Chinese military police. They came over and revealed that this officer was a captain in the military police. George thought he was in hot water for making trouble for the captain, but they quickly found that he was in the wrong place; he was not supposed to be in this apartment. So George finally got rid of him. This was typical of the confusion at that time in Shanghai.

George was told by the American authorities that he had to leave Shanghai or stay at his own peril. They gave the family a few days to get their things together. George filled a couple of suitcases and left everything that he owned in the apartment. His son was six years old, and his daughter was two years old. The family was transferred to a former French Barracks on Route Joseph Frelupt in the French concession. From there they were taken to the airport and flown to Tokyo, Japan.

Like so many others, George and Nadia came to Northern China and Shanghai in the 1920s and left more than twenty-five years later. The only fragments of their thirty years in the Orient were a few mementos and some personal photographs. There were a couple of Chinese statues broken in transit, a few cups and small bottles, a Chinese robe and some Chinese slippers.

After George and Nadia left Shanghai, for the next thirty years under Mao and the Red Guard, Shanghai became stagnant as a metropolis. In their attempts to wipe clean the last whispers of the hundred years of foreign occupation, cruelty and discrimination, the Communists caused the city to fade. Meanwhile, Hong Kong—which had been a sleepy, colonial outpost of the British Empire—blossomed after World War II and expanded into an international metropolitan sensation. Along with Singapore, Hong Kong became a business phenomenon in the East.

When Hong Kong was returned to the Chinese in the '90s, it was apparent that the Communists were impressed with what a city could become both as a business center and as an attraction for world wealth. By then Mao was dead and the Red Guard a bad memory. Very quickly, Shanghai experienced phenomenal growth into a skyscraper metropolis. Now, along with Tokyo, it has again become the greatest city in the Far East.

But the world has lost the old Shanghai. Little more than memories are left of the gathering places and the wanderers that made the city such a tantalizing destination in the years between the great wars. George and Nadia never lost their love of the Orient and the exotic and special place that occupied so much of their youth.

Chapter 33

Memories of China

My childhood memories of China revolve around the property where we lived. I remember that some of the streets were cobblestone and there was a high brick wall that surrounded the property. I was later told our home was part of a complex of buildings that included several multi-story apartment buildings in the International District of Shanghai. The compound of apartments and houses behind a tall brick wall separated the Europeans from the rest of the population.

There were beggars along the brick wall and even women giving birth in the alleys nearby. It was not uncommon to see Chinese walking along the street outside the compound and peeing in the gutters as they walked. Spitting was a popular pastime done with great finesse. As a child I was fascinated when a Chinese would block one nostril and send a projectile from the other for a record breaking distance. It's amazing the things that stay with you as a child.

One day my mother Nadia was so upset by the condition of one young girl living in the streets nearby that she took her in, washed and cared for her. The girl had so many lice in her hair, her scalp was bleeding.

The apartment compound had a large courtyard where children could play under the watchful eye of the Chinese nanny. Every household had cooks and maids. Only a limited number of Chinese entered the compound. I remember my Chinese nanny, my 'amah,' wearing the traditional blue outfit and slacks of the time.

Our family and friends lived in the Russian Quarters, a housing complex populated primarily by Europeans from Russia, Armenia, Eastern Europe, etc.

Nadia and the Chinese Amah

George told me that at one point we lived above the theater that he managed, but I don't remember it. We must have moved to the enclosed compound after George had managed the theater for some time because we were in the compound when my sister was born.

Our apartment had a winding staircase and when I was four years old, I nearly broke my neck falling down those winding stairs trying to slide down the banister. My mother told me that she once caught me finger-painting on the outside of the frosted windows on the top floor. She snuck up on me and pulled me inside to safety.

At the time she was seven months pregnant with my sister, so we must have been there for several seasons. There was a long road that led up to the entrance of the compound and wandering beyond it was dangerous. I wandered outside the compound one day and got bitten by a stray dog suspected of having rabies. I was given twelve shots in the stomach as a preventative.

I remember that my sister Nina was brought home from the hospital in a rickshaw. The rickshaw stopped at the entrance to the compound and my mother got out and showed me Nina for the first time, bundled in a blanket. I was soon trying to make friends with the baby by feeding her a large chocolate bar. My mother stopped me just in time.

One of my family's best friends owned a chain of bakeries in Shanghai and had a grand apartment next door. In the days before they had to evacuate, I remember walking over to their house. Victor and Nina were godparents to my sister Nina and were very friendly with me.

However, when I got to their place one particular day there were boxes and suitcases everywhere. I remember playing hide-and-seek among the luggage they had dragged out in order to pack for the exodus. Victor became very upset with me for messing up his things and sent me home, where I found my own parents packing, too.

I was told that I couldn't take anything with me, especially my toys. So I went into the courtyard and left all my toys with my little Chinese friends.

I even remember that my favorite was a large boat that looked like an ocean liner. I gave it to my best friend when I said goodbye. George and Nadia packed everything that they could fit into their suitcases, literally stuffing the fragments of their life while leaving everything they could not carry behind.

Once again, they were on the run.

From China to Japan to Tubabao

Mao now controlled the mainland of China, which later became the People's Republic of China. However, the PRC was not acknowledged as a country for many years.

Despite having accepted direct help from the Russian Communists and the Russian's goal of controlling China from Moscow, Mao had his own plans for China. Meanwhile, the Americans continued to support Chang Kai-shek.

America did not want to acknowledge the PRC as the official government of China. Once you give a country official status by defining its borders, you can set up treaties for trade, establish embassies, exchange diplomats and officially be recognized as a country.

However, there can be no diplomatic relations with an unrecognized country. As long as various nations did not acknowledge the PRC, citizens of

China abroad were considered displaced people with no legal status. Those of us who were born in the Orient or had lived there all our lives were now non-citizens.

In 1949, the Americans who had helped drive out the Japanese brought warships and aircraft to Shanghai to move the Europeans and Russians who wanted to leave China. Our family got to ride on a military aircraft, courtesy of General Douglas MacArthur. In fact, there were small placards everywhere that read, "Courtesy of General MacArthur."

When we arrived in Japan, we saw these placards all over Tokyo in restaurants, public houses, and shops. The family was flown to Japan and given accommodations at an American military base forty miles outside of Tokyo. The Japanese were still under American occupation. MacArthur controlled everything in the Pacific.

Many of the people who moved from China were headed for UN tent camps set up for the undocumented. There were many such camps across the globe where people were waiting to return to their homeland. But a large majority of the thousands of refugees from China were Russians and eastern Europeans. Most of them did not want to return to the Soviet Union.

Letters sent from relatives contained coded messages warning that those who returned could be sent to prison by the Communists as suspected traitors or spies. Many Russians and eastern Europeans in Europe and the United States had been forcibly returned to the Soviets just after the war. By now stories were coming from behind the iron curtain that these people had disappeared. Some people committed suicide to avoid returning to Communist control.

The Philippine government agreed to establish a UN camp specific to the people leaving China—those who were seeking asylum from the Soviets. Undocumented people were called DPs, displaced persons; they had no travel papers of any kind or were not recognized as part of any country. China after the Communist takeover was officially considered under the control of the Russian Communists.

As part of political pressure against the Communists, China was no longer considered China. The official Chinese government recognized by the Allies was on the island of Formosa, controlled by General Chang Kai-shek. Formosa later became known as Taiwan.

General Douglas MacArthur was in Japan after World War II and gave many displaced persons permission to go to Japan for processing. Our family stayed in Japan for one month and then was flown to the Philippine Islands. I remember flying over the jungle and wondering whether I might see Tarzan swinging from the trees below.

For a youngster it was all very exciting; for the adults, it was one worry after the other.

Chapter 34

The Camp on Tubabao

In 1949 the family went to the island of Tubabao, which is next to the southern tip of Samar Island in the Philippines and connected to other islands by a bridge. Samar is the easternmost island in the Visayas in central Philippines and Tubabao is directly south. The nearest town and airport was Guinan, located on another island about fifteen miles from Tubabao.

The Philippine government had agreed to set aside this island for refugees from the Orient. Undocumented refugees were required to stay in a resettlement camp until a country would take them.

Tubabao is the name of the island and camp village set up by the United Nations to help displaced persons from the Chinese mainland. The nearest military base was Calliquan Base, with an airfield and a bridge. In fact there were bridges that connected several of the small islands. The people in the camp needed official permission to leave the island of Tubabao since they really belonged nowhere.

The camp was run by the International Refugee Organization, the IRO, and was a transfer point for thousands of displaced people, mostly Russians from China. From there some would go to South American countries, some to the Dominican Republic. Many people went to Australia. In fact, by 1951 Australia had accepted 17,000 displaced persons.

George was told that if he wished, the Australian Mission would be glad to take him and his family to Australia. George had become well acquainted with the Consul General for the Australian Mission. His ability with languages made him valuable to the Australians when it came time to load people aboard the ships. The Australian Consul General, who became a good friend, came to George prior to departure.

The Tent Camp on Tubabao

He said, "George, we will hold the ship. Let's go to Australia."

But George told him, "Thank you very much for your kindness. I appreciate your offer, but it's the U.S.A. for me, no matter how long it takes."

So the family stayed behind and waited in the tent camp.

At first there was nothing in the camp but a clearing near the beach and piles of raw supplies. Officials told the refugees to take tents and set them up as best they could to organize the camp. People were divided into groups according to their skills and soon began construction. Single people lived in small tents, while families were given bigger tents. Very soon the camp organizers provided facilities for sanitation, electrical and water management, then police and administration.

Everyone had to work and no one was paid. The IRO provided everything from food, water and toilets, to medical supplies for the tent hospital. Most of the Filipino people on the island were wonderful, setting up a shanty village with shack stores to trade with the refugees. The Filipinos and the refugees even helped set up a restaurant and a church.

Camp administrators appointed counselors to watch over the children and propose activities. They organized everything from parties to explorer treks for the camp children. It was a very successful communal living arrangement, all subsidized by the United Nations.

Chapter 35

The Archbishop of Tubabao

The island of Tubabao in the Philippines is in the path of seasonal monsoons that come in from the Pacific Ocean. During the monsoon season heavy rainstorms are common. Even without a typhoon, which is a hurricane at sea, the seasonal rain would fall like sheets of water from a hose. It could rain for several days with no relief. Nadia remembered seeing the island natives lash themselves to the trees with ropes during a bad storm to avoid being blown out to sea.

The natives and the refugees were always afraid of typhoons. These Pacific storms could wipe out the entire tent camp in one night if it came across the island.

As people arrived they would look at the tent village and express their fears of the typhoons. But the Filipinos (and many of the resident Russians) told everyone that a 'holy man' prayed each night and blessed the camp on all four sides, so there was no reason to be concerned.

The 'holy man' was the Archbishop of Shanghai, who was in the camp running the church and praying for the refugees. He was called Vladyka John, a term of endearment and affection. His actual name and title was Michael Maximovich, Archbishop of Shanghai.

Michael was born in 1896 in the province of Kharkov in Southern Russia. His parents sent him to law school in Kharkov, where he was a gifted student. After a short time he decided to study what he called the spiritual sciences. After the Russian Revolution, he and his family left Russia and in 1926 he became a monk. He was given the name John in honor of a recent canonized saint in Russia. Soon after that he became a teacher at the Seminary of St. John the Theologian at Bitol, Serbia.

It was as a priest and teacher that he was first recognized as a dedicated ascetic. He refused to sleep in a bed and slept only a few hours at a time in a chair or sitting in the corner on the floor. For most of the night, he prayed or walked about the seminary making sure everyone was secure. He rarely wore shoes, and when he did, they were soft slippers with no socks. He wore clothing of the cheapest fabric. At the age of thirty-eight he was sent to Shanghai to unify the community of Russian immigrants there. During his ten years in Shanghai, he rose to the rank of bishop and was instrumental in establishing the Russian Cathedral in Shanghai.

In 1949, when the Chinese Communists took over Shanghai, many Russian immigrants were forced to flee to the Philippines or return to the Soviet Union. By the time he left Shanghai, Vladyka John was elevated to archbishop and recognized as a miracle worker for his countless healings.

He would later travel to America to petition the U.S. Congress to provide visas for the refugees of Tubabao. It was ultimately his personal appeal to the American Congress and the Intervention of the World Church Service that secured permission for thousands of refugees on Tubabao to immigrate to America and Australia.

While he was on the island, the archbishop or his clergy would walk the camp each night and provide a blessing to protect the people on the tiny island. During the twenty-seven months of the camp's existence, only one typhoon threatened the camp, and this storm bypassed the island. After the camp had been evacuated and Vladyka John permanently moved to San Francisco, a terrible typhoon struck the area in the next hurricane season and completely obliterated all the buildings in the abandoned Tubabao camp.

Vladyka John took ill in 1966 while on an Archpastoral visit to Seattle, Washington, and died peacefully soon after. Because of the numerous miracles worked by God through his intercession and prayer, he was canonized and has been elevated to sainthood.

Chapter 36

The First Run Cinema on Tubabao

O ver a period of two years there were many amenities added to the Tubabao village to make life tolerable for the thousands of refugees. Most were necessities, though the most enjoyable luxury was a first-run cinema, a movie house on stilts in the plaza of the tent village. First-run movies were shown regularly on the island even before being released on the American mainland. But there is a story of how a movie house came to be built in the middle of a jungle on a tiny island in the tropics by a couple of enterprising fellows from China. It brought entertainment to thousands of refugees at a time of high anxiety as displaced people waited years for permission to immigrate.

Val Sobel and George became reacquainted on the Philippine Islands in Tubabao. Val was a tall lean fellow with a chiseled, handsome face and a charming personality. On the island, Val was always in the company of young women. In Shanghai he had also had a reputation with the ladies that he encouraged. He had managed the Paris Theater in a seedy part of Shanghai, a place not to be confused with a family establishment. It had a huge dark balcony where theater goers came for more than just the movies. Drunkenness and drug dealing were a few of the activities rumored to be taking place on its balcony.

George and Val both had experience running theaters in Shanghai; George managed the Chikan Theater and Val ran the Paris. But Val hadn't included that information in the records he'd filed with the UN mission. Possibly he believed that his management of the Paris Theater would not serve him well when the security people reviewed his application for immigration. In any event, the UN mission did not know much about Val Sobel and his theatrical management expertise.

First run cinema of Tubabao

But they were aware that George had been the manager of a theater in Shanghai. It was in their records that he knew about projectors, audio equipment and cinema electronics.

The director of the camp was a Captain Combs. No one knew what kind of captain he was, but he ran the camp. An alcoholic, he drank heavily most of the time. The Senior Director of the whole operation was a Captain Pierce, who lived in Manila. Pierce would fly back and forth from Manila to Tubabao regularly to see how things were going.

One day the Senior Director brought a Degree projector—a large, six fold output projector with a small speaker in the lid. All of a sudden, at nine o'clock in the evening, George was told they wanted to see him in the office.

When he arrived, Captain Pierce handed over the projector and said, "I want you to show some movies in the camp."

Captain Pierce, who had brought the projector over to the camp from Manila, said that he knew George had run a large movie house in China. He asked if it would be possible to use the projector to show movies for the refugees.

George said, "How the hell can I show movies with this projector when there's no place to set up and run them?"

The captain gave the projector to George and told the director to help find a place for the movies. Then he left for Manila, expecting George to find a way to make it all happen.

Conferring with his pal Val Sobel, he said, "Val, let's show movies here on Tubabao."

Val thought it was a crazy idea but he was willing to help. No one in the camp really worked much since everything was provided by the IRO. This gave him something to do. They quickly realized that they needed a lot of additional materials besides the projector and began to make a list for the camp director. First they obtained a white canvas to make a screen. Near the camp was a large open-air expanse that could serve as a plaza, which they requisitioned to be used on a regular basis as a theater. Next they took some lumber, put the screen on a wooden frame and hoisted it up on ropes. But, when they tried to show a picture outside using the projector, they found that the sound was lousy, because the speakers were tiny and the projector was exposed to the weather.

George spoke with Captain Combs: "How about we get some decent speakers?"

Combs contacted Captain Pierce in Manila, and Captain Pierce sent over some Johnson 16-inch speakers. Almost as soon as the speakers arrived, George and Val began to make other demands. "You can't just hang speakers without baffles and insulation." They also needed to build a projection booth to protect the projector from the weather. They told Captain Combs that they'd need a lot more supplies than were available in the camp. In particular, they needed lumber and electrical equipment.

Captain Combs told them that there was no lumber at the camp, but there was lots of lumber and supplies at the Calliquan Base, not far from the town of Tubabao. He authorized them to go to the base and pick up whatever was needed.

At the base they just couldn't believe what was available. There were refrigerators on top of refrigerators, stoves, replacement parts of all kinds, car supplies, furniture, and finished wood. Filipino guards protected the yard, because everything imaginable could be found inside the base fence.

They found long boxes made of polished wood that were at least four by six feet. In the boxes were roofing materials, nails, tools, and everything else they needed. To build their projection booth, all they had to do was tell the guard how many boxes and what kind of supplies they needed. They had authorization, so no questions were asked. Everything was assumed to be required for the military. They went to the motor pool for a truck, and after figuring out how many boxes they required to build a projection booth, they loaded the boxes on the truck and went back to the camp.

Now they had polished wood, nails and tools. They made a frame for the screen, put up the screen, and began building the booth. With so much material available, they decided to build more than just a booth. The projection booth evolved into a small house with an interior large enough for several people to sit comfortably and run the equipment. It was built on stilts several feet off the ground because of the heavy rains that came through the area. They built containment boxes for the sixteen-inch Johnson speakers, and they requested—and were given—army blankets, which they set up inside the boxes as baffles.

On either side of the screen they created a pulley system so that they could lift the speaker boxes up high. In case of rain large canvases that fit over the speakers and the screen could be erected quickly.

After finishing the project, they still didn't like the sound system. The problem wasn't the quality, but the lack of power. The amplifiers had only six watts and were not sufficiently powerful to broadcast for a large area. They went back to the base, acquired some twenty-watt amplifiers, and rigged up the necessary electronics to give them powerful speakers.

The Americans in Manila had first-run feature movies flown in from Hollywood for the Army personnel every week. These were featurettes, cartoons and full-length movies that were produced in Hollywood and provided to the troops even before the general public saw them. Captain Pierce made arrangements to have the movies flown to Tubabao for the little theater.

Thanks to the American military, Hollywood, and an Armenian entrepreneur named George and his friend Val, the colony of 5,000 refugees enjoyed MGM musicals and other first-run features like *Pinocchio* and *Samson and Delilah* before they were released on the mainland. The audience brought their own folding chairs and set them up in the plaza lot.

Once a week, George would take a smaller screen, the projector and one of the speakers to the hospital and run movies for the patients and staff.

Usually, George would just sit in the projection booth and run the equipment. The projection booth was large enough to accommodate a few seats for VIPs. These included George's family, Val Sobel and his girlfriends, members of the American Mission, Donald White, Captain Combs and a few others. Everyone else had to sit in the open air plaza.

The two entrepreneurs decorated the outside of the projection booth with movie posters and movie artwork. Val and George ran the movie house for nearly two years while they were living on the island waiting for permission to enter America.

Chapter 37

Memories of Tubabao

It is interesting the things one recalls from childhood—the things that make a lasting impression. After all these years, I still remember the giant tents set up near the jungle at the edge of the village, the heat and humidity, the rain that made everything so slick, the mosquito netting and the bugs. During the dry season, there was lots of dust and everyone went outside in the hot sun. During the wet season, there was lots of mud and everyone stayed under cover. And yet, none of the details of the village itself stayed with me.

For example, I don't remember the beach or the ocean, though it couldn't have been very far from the tent village. And the ocean reefs in that part of the world must be spectacular. I was told there was a Filipino village set up by the IRO—a row of shacks and stores—not far from the tent village. But even that seems like a blur.

It is possible that as a child I could not distinguish between the IRO village and the Filipino village, though I'm sure they were very different. There are photographs showing me under the watchful eye of the counselors in a Boy Scout outfit and participating in parties with all the other children in the camp. But I have no memories of any of this, so it must not have made an impression. However, other things are very clear.

The most powerful memories of the tent village have to do with sleeping under that mosquito net. Somehow, for a child, having a huge finely woven net strung over a canopy and completely enclosing the bed must have been distinctive. There were countless folds in the netting and it hung like fine silk and moved with the slightest breeze. The netting was of course the principal defense against all the bugs that might come in from the jungle each night. Every morning a caring mother or grandmother would check for bugs before the children left their beds.

There were other memories of the jungle itself. It was a grand playground with cleared paths leading deep into the greenery. In some sections it was a huge canopy that blocked out the sun. There were monkeys in the trees. Exotic plants like elephant palms with leaves as large as people grew along the paths. Fruit trees seemed to be everywhere, especially bananas trees.

The Filipino villagers and the refugees would go into the jungle to harvest bananas, bringing back heavy bunches of green bananas on their shoulders.

Apparently the fruit grew so prolifically and the villagers had cultivated the trees so successfully that bunches of bananas could be harvested from the same area several times a year.

The rainy season was spectacular. Rain on the island came down as sheets of water with a heavy mist rising from the ground making everything slippery. The Filipino children would find cardboard boxes left unattended and use the cardboard in the rain to slide along any bare patch of ground as if skiing on snow.

How to Catch a Monkey with a Bottle

When I was a child, the monkeys in the trees held a particular fascination for me. Most were small brown monkeys, probably rhesus, and they were constantly jumping from limb to limb and chattering to one another. One day my dad's friend, Val Sobel, saw me staring at the monkeys up in the trees.

He came over and said, "One of the Filipinos tells me that he can catch a monkey with a bottle. Would you like to try?"

I must have looked very puzzled. How did you catch a monkey with a bottle? Val insisted that he could catch one of the monkeys and make it into a pet.

For several days, Val kept teasing me about the secret skill of catching a monkey with a bottle. Actually I think he was as intrigued with the idea as I was, so when I begged him to do it, he finally agreed to try.

The next day he brought over one of the Filipino villagers and the necessary ingredients. The most crucial ingredient was the bottle itself—one of those small individual milk bottles with a narrow neck, not the bigger quart bottles, but the smaller ones popular in those days. The Filipino cleaned and polished the milk bottle so it would catch the sunlight. Then he dropped in several handfuls of raisins or fruit. He tied a strong twine around the neck of the bottle and tied the other end to a tree not far from where the monkeys were playing.

We sat out of sight for what seemed like hours, watching the little bottle. The monkeys could see the bottle sparkling on the ground and, like all curious animals, came down to investigate.

They also could see the raisins. Soon, one or two of them approached the bottle to get a closer look. It seemed that none of them would ever be brave enough to touch it.

Finally, one brave little fellow came over to the bottle, stuck in his small paw, grabbed a few raisins and ran. He must have liked the raisins because a few moments later he approached the bottle again and put his paw in for another, bigger handful.

Suddenly the Filipino jumped up and started yelling and running toward the monkey. The monkey on the ground and all his companions in the trees started chattering and screaming; however, the little monkey on the ground kept jumping and running around in circles, as if unable to get away from the bottle. At last the Filipino was able to corner the monkey and drop a brown cloth bag over his body and head. In a flash the monkey was inside the bag.

Apparently the monkey had reached into the bottle to grab the raisins and, frightened by all the noise, had made a fist, making it impossible for him to pull his paw out of the narrow neck bottle to escape. The more the Filipino frightened the monkey, the tighter the little fellow's fist. He couldn't get free because the bottle was tied to the tree.

My parents found out almost immediately that we had captured a monkey and insisted we release it. Despite my pleading and crying, they made it clear that there was no way we could keep a pet in the tent village.

Why the Pythons were Hung Up in the Trees

Another memorable experience with animals on the island had to do with a giant snake. There were many dangerous animals in the Philippine jungle—scorpions, centipedes, bats. Black scorpions could be found in decaying material on the jungle floor. No one ever looked for them other than to avoid them. They couldn't kill but could make you very sick. Giant centipedes were also common. They didn't look dangerous, but the Filipinos warned the refugees that the centipedes would cause a terrible infection if you touched them.

Bats could be seen at dusk, but they did not bother people much. The giant snakes, however, were something else altogether.

Pythons in that part of the world can grow to be ten feet long and are perfectly capable of grabbing a small dog, a village pig or even a child. I don't remember ever seeing the other dangerous animals, but I do remember one particular snake. One day, I must've wandered into the Filipino shanty village or perhaps followed people who were excited about something. All I do remember is that there was a large group of people gathering in one section of the village—the Filipino village, not the tent village. Someone had killed a large python and hung it in a tree near the edge of the village. People were standing around it and admiring the kill.

I asked one of the older Filipino boys why the snake was hanging from the tree, and he said, "It is a warning to all the other snakes to stay away."

Now I am sure this is a possible reason but I think a more likely explanation is that the snake was hanging from the tree because it was being prepared for a rather exotic meal. I didn't stick around to find out.

I spent nearly two years on that island. I don't remember any schooling or any of the organized activities. None of that was as important as the jungle, the monkey, the snake, the tent city, the beach and the cinema. But mostly I remember the cinema.

I remember sitting in my father's lap peeking through an opening in the projection booth and watching cartoons and feature films in the cinema that George and Val had created. Everything on the island was a grand adventure for a nine year old.

Chapter 38

Leaving the Island

The family remained on the island until the U.S. mission was organized and started processing people for entrance into the United States. George was useful to the Americans since he could speak several languages. Many times the American Mission would bring George in to help translate and process people for immigration. This gave George an opportunity to be in a position to immigrate to the U.S. as soon as a sponsor became available.

Everyone who wanted to go to the United States had to have a sponsor. The sponsor signed an affidavit—sometimes called an assurance—with the government. More than half the people in the camp had no friends or relatives in America to sign such an assurance. They had to rely on charitable organizations or church affiliations to gain admission. In simplest terms a sponsor was responsible for making sure that the immigrant was not a burden on the economy. The sponsor made a written commitment to meet the immigrant, arrange for lodging, teach the immigrant local customs, language and, most important, how to get a job. This obligation lasted for a whole year at least and sometimes as long as five.

In addition, the immigrant was required to sign a sworn statement that he or she had never been convicted of a felony, had no communicable diseases and had never been a member of any un-American organization such as Communists or Nazis. The American Mission screened each applicant carefully and used Army and OSS information obtained during the war to determine if any of the potential immigrants were lying.

Soon after the mission started to process people, George began to serve as a translator for one of the immigration officers, Donald White. Officer White had a special tent fitted with a desk and several file cabinets. George would sit in during interviews and help people answer the officer's questions. George remembered one particular interview that served as an example of how thorough the American Mission was in determining whether an immigrant was qualified to come to America.

George always suspected that Donald White was more than just an immigration officer. He believed that White was either a high ranking military officer or working for the OSS. In 1945 George had worked as a translator in Shanghai for the American military and knew how the intelligence officers operated.

And now he was helping Donald White on the island with interviews of refugees. During one such session, Officer White was interviewing a tall slender man with a beard, who was from Eastern Europe, possibly Ukraine or Poland. George was there because the man's English was poor, but could understand Russian.

At one point in the interview Officer White asked, "Have you ever been convicted of any crimes or been in prison?"

"No," the slender man replied.

Officer White noticed that the man had a very heavy beard. "Have you always had that beard?" asked Officer White. "Yes, since I was a young man," answered the refugee.

At which point Officer Donald White opened a drawer and pulled out a file. He looked for a moment at what was obviously a large photograph.

Then he showed the picture to the slender man and told George to ask him one final question.

"Are you the man in this photograph?" was the question. The photograph showed the slender man, but he had no beard and was wearing a prison uniform. The man looked at the photograph and began to cry. He knew he was not going to America.

How the photograph came to Officer White and how Officer White made the connection to this man was never discovered. But George saw several such interviews end with similar evidence that came from the files in that tent.

Nadia Stays Behind

George found a sponsor and finally won approval for his family to go to America; unfortunately, Nadia was not allowed to go with them. George received word that she was refused entry because of medical reasons. Apparently, during a routine medical examination required by the US Mission, an X-ray revealed a small tuberculin cyst. Nadia was admitted to a tuberculosis ward in the island hospital, where she was required to stay in quarantine.

She would not be allowed to emigrate. Actually it should not be a surprise that Nadia, showing signs of tuberculosis, was denied a permit to enter. One must remember that this was the early 1950s. Sovereignty of the country was considered sacred. Strict immigration laws required strict screening processes. No one with a criminal record would be allowed into the United States. No one with a suspected communicable disease. No one affiliated with a political organization that was anti-American. And no one objected. There were no protests or appeals. That was the procedure and everyone understood the rules.

On the island, in addition to George and Nadia, the family consisted of Nadia's mother (Arpenik) and father (Haig), an eight-year-old son (Ed) and a four-year-old daughter (Nina). They all had a single sponsor who had signed one assurance for the family. But the family was devastated.

Nadia and George sat together and discussed everything. They both felt that the family might not get another chance to go to the United States.

The choice was simple but painful. Either they all stayed together on the island and tried to go to the U.S. later, or Nadia would have to stay behind while the rest of the family left. Nadia was confident she would get well again and somehow join us at some point in the future. She and George decided that the family would go on to America while she stayed behind in the hospital indefinitely.

To San Francisco

The family was put on board an army transport provided again by General MacArthur, who handled all traffic across the Pacific. The transport was called the General Haan. During the crossing from the Philippines to the West Coast of the United States, the ship passed through a Pacific typhoon. All the adults were sick and frightened, while the children thought storm was yet another fun filled adventure.

As stated earlier, George was in a particularly good position and on very good terms with the American Mission, because he helped them translate and process the immigrants. In particular, he was acquainted with the immigration officer Donald White.

Officer White, who was in a position to know, told George, "George, just because you're going to the United States, you are not in the United States yet. After they put their stamp on your papers and legally admit you—then you will be in the United States."

Because of his ability with languages, even on board the ship George was repeatedly engaged by the American Mission as a translator to explain all the proper procedures to other passengers. As strange as it may seem, while the immigrants were out at sea for eighteen days, information on the people on board was still coming in. When they all arrived in San Francisco, George had the unfortunate responsibility of having to tell some of the people that, because of the latest information received, they would not be allowed to disembark. The authorities took them away and George did not know what became of them. *Just because you're going to America doesn't mean you're in the United States yet.*

After eighteen days of travel on board the army transport, the family arrived in San Francisco. The date was January 25, 1951. Instead of staying in San Francisco, George wanted to continue on; he had convinced himself that the family needed to be near the person who sponsored the family for immigration to the United States.

George had received a letter from the sponsor while on Tubabao the previous year and so had an address. The sponsor was living in Chicago, Illinois, and so the family traveled from San Francisco to Chicago, where they coincidentally settled in an apartment on Chicago Avenue.

Chapter 39

Nadia's Vision

About ten months later, while in the isolation ward in the hospital, Nadia had what she felt was a prophetic dream, a vision. She dreamt that the Blessed Mother had appeared to her. In the dream Nadia asked her when she could be with her family again. The Blessed Mother Mary smiled and said, "Soon."

When she awakened from the dream, Nadia begged the doctors to take more X-rays. The doctors had been monitoring her condition and saw no need for an unscheduled examination. Even though they were skeptical, they finally agreed. They quickly realized that the tuberculin cyst or spot had mysteriously vanished.

Since they couldn't find any evidence of a communicable disease, they had to release her from the hospital. An appeal was made for Nadia to join her family in America. And so, after nearly a year's delay, Nadia was finally cleared and allowed to proceed to the United States. Her telegram to America was brief and heartfelt: "Passed medical, waiting Visa, Love Mama Nadia."

She arrived in San Francisco in November of 1951 and was greeted by her old friends from Shanghai, Victor and Nina. The last time she had seen them was in Shanghai during the exodus. They welcomed her into their new San Francisco home.

To Chicago by Train

To allow Nadia to join her family, George had sent money to pay for Nadia to take a plane to Chicago. But their friend Nina was very concerned about flying. She thought it was much too dangerous, especially in foggy November.

The City of Los Angeles

(Western History Department of The Denver Public Library – OP-17407)

She convinced Nadia to use the money to take the train instead.

"The train is so much nicer." Nina told her friend. "You can sleep, read, see the countryside, the mountains covered in snow. You will arrive in three days, relaxed and refreshed."

It seemed ideal and Nadia decided to take a train from San Francisco to Chicago on a modern diesel train called the 'City of San Francisco.'

The telegram from her friend Nina was a simple announcement of the change in plans. "Good news, Nadia left Oakland Station at 5:30 on SP Train #102. Will arrive in Chicago North Western Station on Tuesday at 10:45 a.m.; Love and Kisses, Nina."

Nadia had communicated where she was and when she would arrive. The family was expecting her. Everything seemed to be working out just fine as she sat in her third car compartment and watched the snow falling outside. She wasn't quite sure where she was but the train was definitely climbing into the mountains of western America.

On November 12, 1951, there was a blinding snowstorm in the Weber Canyon in the Wasatch Mountains of southwest Wyoming.

The conditions were reported to be so bad, the crew of the fourteen-car flyer 'City of Los Angeles', a diesel-powered train out of L.A., had decided to stop in the Weber Canyon. There was traffic ahead and they were unable to see the posted snow-covered safety block signals. Both the Streamliner City of San Francisco and the Flyer City of Los Angeles were eastbound for Chicago on the same track. They were running approximately thirty minutes apart.

Suddenly, about four miles west of Evanston, Wyoming, the City of San Francisco ripped four car lengths into the City of Los Angeles, first smashing into its observation car and laying it open onto the snow. The other three cars were demolished by the onrushing three-section diesel locomotive. The impact derailed all eleven cars of the City of San Francisco, many of which jackknifed across the right-of-way into a freight train parked on an adjacent siding. The front cars of the second train, about half of that streamliner, remained on the tracks.

Rescue efforts were started at once, but were hampered considerably by all the snow in the canyon and the freezing temperatures. Workers removed the injured and dead from the wreck all day and through the night, aided by huge floodlights. Most of the 3,800 residents of Evanston turned out to assist in the rescue work and ease the suffering of the victims.

Forty-nine injured persons were transported to Uinta County Memorial Hospital at Evanston by bus, ambulance, truck and automobile along nearby Route 30.

All the dead passengers were aboard the City of Los Angeles, which had originally carried fifty-three people. None of the 150 passengers on the City of San Francisco were seriously injured, but several had been trapped in the wreckage. On the day of the accident fourteen bodies were taken to the Evanston morgues; at that time six more dead were visible inside. The dead included two physicians, part of a medical group that had attended American Medical Association conventions in San Francisco; all the uninjured doctors aboard the trains pitched in to assist the local medics. Dead crewmen including the electrician employed on the City of San Francisco, its rear brakeman, two porters, and a club car attendant on the City of Los Angeles.

Two days later rescue workers cut through the last of the two-train debris with acetylene torches and eventually recovered all the bodies. The cause of the accident was attributed to the severe snowstorm, which had reduced visibility to near zero and blocked out the warning lights.

In the absence of definite signals to proceed, it was believed that the crew of the City of San Francisco should have stopped or proceeded with greater caution, knowing that the other streamliner was running ahead and that there was only a limited margin of travel time between the two trains.

Nadia was on board the City of San Francisco when it collided with the City of Los Angeles. She was in the third car, in a compartment that became sealed by the collision. Although the crew had been killed or severely injured, the passengers managed to walk away from the trains relatively unharmed. However, the *Chicago Tribune* newspaper reported the derailment and the family was frantic to find out what had happened. Nadia's father Haig was displaying all the symptoms of a heart attack. They would not hear anything for two days.

Rescuers reached the compartment and cut it open with a torch. After

Train Survivors Reach Here on Wreck Special

Scores of relatives and friends who had waited into the night were at the North Western Station early today for the arrival of 40 Chicago area victims of the Union Pacific train wreck near Evanston, Wyo., Monday.

The victims arrived on a special North Western train, flying a white flag and bearing the numbers of the two wrecked trains, 104 for the City of Los Angeles and 102 for the City of San Francisco.

VANDERBILTS IN WRECK

Among the 75 passengers from other areas were George Vanderbilt, grandson of the late Commodore Cornelius Vanderbilt, and his wife, Anita.

Mrs. Vanderbilt said:

"The accident was too horrible to describe."

The Vanderbilts were on the last car of the City of San Francisco, the train that rammed the City of Los Angeles, and were only shaken up.

Relatives of Dr. Anthony S. Ippolito and his wife, Camille, awaited arrival of their bodies. They will be taken to the Iarussi chapel, 619 S. Ashland av. Funeral arrangements were being made.

One of the most joyful reunions was that between Mrs. Nadejda Sergoyan, 32, and her husband, George, and their two children, Edward, 8, and Nina, 4, of 1372 W. Chicago av.

INTERNED BY JAPS

Mrs. Sergoyan was coming from the Philippine Islands aboard the train from San Francisco to join her husband, who came here last January with the children.

Armenians who had been living in China when World War II broke out, they were interned by the Japanese for several years.

Newspaper article after Nadia's safe arrival in Chicago

she was released her from the wreckage, Nadia was dazed, bruised and in shock—but not seriously injured. The rescuers had more critically injured to find and treat. Unattended, Nadia began to wander in the snow. She was having difficulty speaking English and wandered about near the train wreck, still wrapped in a rescue blanket.

At last she was picked up near the highway by the medics and moved into town to a hotel. While she showed no signs of physical injury, there was some concern about shock and trauma because she was constantly crying. She sat in the hotel room all night and all the next day.

Finally a good Samaritan noticed her crying and asked, "Are you hurt? Why are you crying?"

Nadia said in broken English, "Telegram, telegram, send telegram." The woman understood and helped her compose a telegram to tell her family that she had survived and would see them soon. It was brief and to the point: "Am not hurt in City San Francisco train wreck, don't know when we leave here—Nadia."

Nadia had been separated from her family for a year, and her four-year-old daughter no longer recognized her. After the family was reunited in Chicago, the little girl kept calling her mother "Auntie." But before too long mother and daughter became reacquainted and they all began their life as a family in America.

Soon after settling in America, Nadia also changed her name to sound more American. Her original name was Nadjesda, which means 'hope' in Russian. Nadia was a less formal version. Once in America, she preferred to be called Nadine and was called Nadine by friends and family for the rest of her life.

After several more days, arrangements were made for Nadia to continue her journey to Chicago, where she was finally reunited with her family. She arrived late in the evening to awaken her children and hold them for the first time since Tubabao. Years later, Nadia told her daughter that during media coverage of her arrival in Chicago was one of the few times in their long marriage when George told her "I love you" in public.

Chapter 40

Life in the U.S.A.

Upon arriving in the United States, as soon as the family was settled, George walked over to Montgomery Ward, a big department store in Chicago. He went up to the loading dock and asked for a job, telling the people there that he would do anything. The boss at the loading dock didn't know what to make of this guy, but he must have been impressed, because George was hired that same day. He became a packer on a conveyor belt, and the pay was $1.25 an hour.

He worked there for a short period of time and then joined another company as a billing clerk for thirty-five cents an hour more. Eventually he advanced to a position of supervisor in the billing and shipping department.

As soon as George had saved enough cash to put a down payment on a house, he bought his first home in America. The realtor arranged a mortgage with a local mortgage manager and on the day the papers were to be signed, George and Nadia arrived to close the deal.

The loan officer greeted the two and said, "We need the down payment to finalize the purchase and then everything will go into escrow. How do you want to make the down payment?"

George opened an old worn leather briefcase and dumped a large sum of cash on the manager's desk. He slowly began to count as the manager caught his breath and kept interrupting with the same question.

"What are you doing? We are not set up to handle cash."

As George continued to count out the cash, he explained, "Well you want the down payment for the house. I have brought the money."

"But why didn't you just bring a check?" asked the manager.

Obviously this banker had never dealt with anyone who did business in

Old Shanghai. Small business matters were handled by check but important purchases in the Orient were always handled in cash, never by personal check. Earlier that day, George had stopped at his bank and insisted on cash from his savings. It took some time for George to trust banks. He had met too many crooks and swindlers in his travels. And it took him a bit longer to learn the American way of credit.

Several more years of hard work passed; then George got into a dispute with the son of his boss, and they decided to go their separate ways. He took his profit sharing and his savings, and he and Nadine opened up a restaurant delicatessen in Chicago.

The couple made investments in real estate, ran several businesses, bought several homes and lived comfortably. George and Nadine finally retired in Seattle, Washington, in 1986.

George in America, 1961

Chapter 41

The Two-Percenters

W hat forms your view of the world? What shapes your attitudes and quirks, your passions and prejudices? Who are the people that influenced you and may have even helped to shape your character?

Because of my education and interests, the famous and near famous on my list of people are an eclectic group chosen mostly from engineering, the sciences and the arts. And yet, the people who have had the greatest influence in my life are all so-called 'common folk' who have only one thing in common: they gathered at one time or another at the Armenian Social Club in Shanghai in the first half of the last century. It was a time of such chaos and tragedy that some have called it the Modern Dark Ages. They were all part of that two percent who traveled the farthest to establish a new life.

Virtually my entire view of the world, attitudes and prejudices, passions and behaviors are shaped by these unusual people, who were brought together in a club I never saw and will never be able to visit.

I have long considered why a club in Shanghai should be so unique, aside from its exotic setting. After all, there were more unusual places in the Orient and this club was not what one would consider a center of excellence by any measure. There must be places more interesting than a club populated by undocumented refugees. And yet this setting seems to have attracted an unusual number of remarkable and motivated individuals.

Perhaps the reason has something to do with attitude. The refugees drawn to this gathering place in Shanghai had something in common with what people now call the American Spirit. This Spirit—an attitude of 'can do' and an unparalleled work ethic—may well have originated with the immigrants whose children and grandchildren are considered one hundred percent American.

What formed this 'American Spirit'? Is it the product of the wilderness experience, the heritage of religious and social persecution, or the absence of Old World restrictions? Early Americans are a ninety-eight percent mix of refugees, whose behavior and attitudes made them distinct from other ethnic groups.

There are two professors of psychiatry who separately published books attributing the unique and exceptional characters of Americans to a new and unsuspected source: American DNA. They argue that the United States is full of energetic risk-takers because it's full of immigrants who as a group may carry a genetic marker that expresses itself as restless curiosity, an almost sophomoric enthusiasm and competitive self-promotion—a combination that they have coined a word to describe: *hypomania*. Peter C. Whybrow of UCLA and John D. Gardner of Johns Hopkins University Medical Center make their case for an immigrant specific genotype in their respective books: *American Mania* and *The Hypomaniac Edge*.

Even when times are hard, Whybrow points out, most people don't leave their homelands. Most people live their entire lives within a fixed radius of their ancestral village. They marry people of similar socio-economic backgrounds and form most of their attitudes and opinions based on the common consensus of the village. They want to belong to the community of their fathers and their fathers' fathers and will suffer any hardship to stay put. Even when displaced by war, they will, at first opportunity, come back to their familiar villages and start again.

But there is in each village a separate two percent. These are the two percent who will endure and overcome any obstacle to leave the village and recreate their lives in another setting. They will leave family, home and familiar surroundings with little but what they can carry. What distinguishes them, Whybrow suggests, might be that pathway in the brain that expresses itself in boldness and novelty seeking. Given an opportunity, they seek a new horizon.

This genetic variation seems to have been disproportionately prevalent in the groups that over generations walked the farthest from their ancestral home—a group never satisfied with the status quo and always seeking something new.

So if the genetic marker cuts across immigrant groups of all origins, it's not about where they came from, it's that they decided to make the journey.

They can be found in frontier regions across all continents, and their unique behavior is a function of both genetics and environment. If these people are placed in a completely unrestricted marketplace, with the 'anything goes' rules of a free marketplace, they thrive. Apparently it is not just the immigrant gene but the immigrant in an unrestricted environment under pressure to succeed that seems to generate a unique spirit. It is not surprising that immigrants in similar unrestrained environments—such as the settlers of Hong Kong, Australia, and the frontiers of Canada and the colonials in Africa—exhibit many of these same characteristics.

However, once a people become passive, or a government makes the environment too comfortable or overly restricted, those people soon become part of the ninety-eight percent of the village who accept a restricted market and a governing authority, and they stay put. That generation then becomes the status quo that does not want to leave, does not want to take risks. They will now suffer any hardship or accept any restriction to stay part of the village. They become complacent.

In Shanghai, in the first half of the twentieth century, complacency was not an option, and there was plenty of stress. There was war, economic depression, revolution, and occupation all flavored by an exotic backdrop. Yet, no matter the obstacles, these people kept their optimistic attitudes. The market was unrestricted and fueled by old world bribery, where any obstacle could be removed for a price.

These conditions helped form the characters of a large community of immigrants. The Japanese who were the occupiers of China at the time recognized and actually encouraged the free market spirit of the immigrants, who had been welcomed to Harbin and later to the free port of Shanghai. The Japanese realized that the free market created by these refugees was bound to thrive.

The immigrants who gathered at the Social Club had common origins and circumstances. And they exhibited similar symptoms, symptoms akin to *hypomania*—a state described as persistent and pervasive elevated moods. People experiencing these symptoms typically have a flood of ideas and mildly grandiose thoughts. Unlike those who suffer from other mood disorders, these people tend to be extremely goal oriented.

This is not to say that these immigrants had delusions or hallucinations. They did not lose touch with reality. They were very rooted in the reality of the day because the reality of the day was often filled with violence and hardship. But these people were generally energetic, euphoric, visionary, charismatic— and sometimes a bit overconfident and outgoing, with poorly developed ideas.

The 'can do' attitude and work ethic that is envied by many may be a general trait common to any group of refugees in a hostile environment who can take advantage of opportunities. That characteristic may have been what made the Social Club in Shanghai unique; it attracted people with a common predisposition to adventure, risk-taking and high expectations, struggling against a backdrop of unprecedented obstacles.

Any club that attracts such people represents a highly skewed and unusual self-selected population. "*Hypomaniacs* are ideally suited by temperament to become immigrants," John Gardner of Johns Hopkins University explains. America has drawn *hypomaniacs* like a magnet for 300 years. It's no wonder that most of the people in the Armenian Social Club viewed America as their personal ultimate destination, no matter what obstacles lay before them. America was seen as a wide-open land with seemingly infinite possibilities. It presented an undeniable attraction for restless, ambitious people who felt hemmed in by their own traditions.

Those of us who inherited that spirit, whether we ultimately wound up in America or elsewhere in the world, were the lucky ones. We were the beneficiaries of some extraordinary people who will exert their influence on us forever.

Epilogue

George and Nadine had two grandchildren. They watched the children grow up into their teen years. Lisa was born in 1976 and Andrenik was born in 1979. Both children had an opportunity to meet and know their grandparents, though they probably did not understand how out of the ordinary these people were and what they endured during their long lives as they provided for their family. Perhaps these stories will help explain these people and provide the next generation of children with insight into their heritage.

Once, during a quiet moment, George confessed that he regarded his grandchildren as his immortality. These stories are dedicated to Lisa and Andrenik and their children.

Many of these stories were taken from audiotape recordings of an interview with George and Nadine. The audiotapes, made in the 1980s, detail their personal remembrances. In many cases I have included extra information and additional commentary from interviews with other contributors.

George died in April of 1991 at the age of seventy-nine. Nadine died eighteen months later, in July of 1992.

E.G. Sergoyan holds degrees in aeronautical and mechanical engineering and has been involved in the aerospace industry for over forty years. Since the days of Apollo he has worked for a variety of aerospace companies and participated in many of the major space research projects. For the past twenty years, Mr. Sergoyan has been a Boeing senior engineer in Seattle, developing technology to improve aircraft manufacturing. He is a Boeing Designated Expert (BDE) in measurement systems and has a dozen patent awards and numerous technical publications. The stories in *The Gathering Place* come from interviews with friends and family. The book is his first non-technical publication. Mr. Sergoyan and his wife live in Mukilteo, Washington, with family nearby. He spends his spare time enjoying the mountains and underwater scenery in the American Northwest, hand knotting oriental rugs on a Tabriz loom, and playing tennis.

www.ingramcontent.com/pod-product-compliance
Lightning Source LLC
Chambersburg PA
CBHW011828020426
42334CB00025B/2973